More Praise for *Ride the River*

"Larry Christenson has a gift for communicating spiritual truths by painting pictures in the reader's imagination, images that stay in the memory for years. In *Ride the River* he has turned the real-life story of Lewis and Clark into a practical parable, an inspiring and informative help in knowing and doing God's will."

Dr. Morris G. C. Vaagenes
North Heights Lutheran Church, St. Paul, Minnesota

"Larry Christenson writes as he has always done—with depth and simplicity. The depth comes from his actual experience of God; the simplicity uses the art of the parable to great effect, as Christ himself did. I recommend this book to all who wish to be guided more clearly in the ways of God."

Father Michael Harper
Antiochian Orthodox Church, Cambridge, England

"It has been my privilege and delight to Ride the River in the company and counsel of Larry for many years. I've always been fed by his sermons, studies, articles, and books—and this one just may be his finest yet. Get wet!"

Paul Anderson
Lutheran Renewal

"For those interested in history, both secular and spiritual, *Ride the River* offers a fascinating look at the Lewis and Clark expedition. As usual with Larry Christenson, the book is well-written and charming. I highly recommend it."

Dr. Vinson Synan
Dean, Regent University School of Divinity

BOOKS BY
LARRY CHRISTENSON

The Christian Family

The Heartless Troll

The Renewed Mind

Ride the River

The Wonderful Way Babies Are Made

Welcome, Holy Spirit

RIDE THE RIVER

LARRY CHRISTENSON

BETHANY HOUSE PUBLISHERS
Minneapolis, Minnesota

Ride the River
Copyright © 2000
Larry Christenson

Cover design: Uttley/DuoPonce DesignWorks
Cover photo: Chad Ehlers. Stone

Except as noted, italics in Scripture quotations and other quotations are the author's.

Published by Bethany House Publishers
A Ministry of Bethany Fellowship International
11400 Hampshire Avenue South, Bloomington, Minnesota 55438
www.bethanyhouse.com

Printed in the United States of America by Bethany Press International

Library of Congress Cataloging-in-Publication Data

Christenson, Larry, 1928–
    Ride the river : experience the full power of a life journey with God / by Larry Christenson.
       p. cm.
    Includes bibliographical references and index.
    ISBN 0–7642–2374–7 (pbk.)
    1. Christian life—Lutheran authors. 2. Trinity. I. Title.
    BV4501.2 .C5142   2000
    248.4'841—dc21   00–010882

Dedicated to
our Corps of Discovery

the people of
Trinity Lutheran Church
San Pedro, California
and two leader-couples

Bob and Greta Scott   Bud and Jean Hahn

We saw the great vistas together
we rode the rapids
we slogged across sandbars of discouragement together
we proceeded on.

LARRY CHRISTENSON is an ordained Lutheran minister, bestselling author, and popular speaker. He has written numerous articles and books, including *The Christian Family* (two million copies sold) and *The Renewed Mind*. He and his wife, Nordis, travel extensively, speaking at conferences, in colleges and seminaries, and in congregations. They make their home in northern Minnesota.

Acknowledgments

During the writing of this book my wife, Nordis, has been my greatest encourager and my best critic. We spent countless hours discussing the ideas and research that went into the book. Her ideas and comments continually helped shape and reshape the manuscript. Someone has said that during the rewrite process writers must be willing to "murder their darlings"—ruthlessly cross out words and phrases they have labored to create, and have become dearly attached to, but which do not advance the book's purpose. Nordis read through every draft of the book with red pencil in hand and helped murder my darlings. No words can express my thanks for the quality and the quantity of her help.

My thanks to Gary and Carol Johnson, at Bethany House Publishers, who first encouraged me to write a book on the theme of divine guidance and empowerment. That was in 1980, so I thank them for their patience!

At a critical stage of the project, four editors and writers read through the manuscript and returned invaluable ideas and suggestions: Dorothy Ranaghan, Debra Christenson, Lois Walfrid Johnson, and Ronald Klug. My thanks to each one of them. My added thanks to Ronald Klug, who subsequently did a thorough edit of the final draft.

My thanks to Jeff Braun, at Bethany House Publishers, who expressed such a personal and lively interest in the book. He took the manuscript under his wing, discussed it with me, and did a fine and final edit.

My final thanks to Bert Mitchell Anderson, the literary consultant and eccentric genius who came into my life many years ago, and did his best to teach me the craft of writing.

CONTENTS

CHAPTER ONE

PURPOSE AND PARABLE

*In which we introduce the theme of this book and a parable from
American history.*

COMING INTO THE twenty-first century, America celebrates a
momentous happening that took place two hundred years ago—
the historic exploration of the American West under the co-command
of Lewis and Clark.

Under the leadership of Meriwether Lewis and William Clark,
the "Corps of Discovery," a hardy band of thirty-two people, accomplished
one of the great explorations in recorded history, a
journey lasting twenty-eight months, covering eight thousand
miles. According to instructions from President Thomas Jefferson,
they rode the Missouri River to its headwaters, crossed the Rocky
Mountains to the Columbia River, and rode that river to its
mouth on the Pacific Ocean, then returned. Jefferson named it a
"Voyage of Discovery."

Throughout the journey, Lewis and Clark shared leadership on
an equal footing. From the first paddle stroke up the Missouri
River the expedition operated with two courageous, competent,
and coequal leaders. If either of them had been missing, the expedition
would have fallen short of its goal.

A Parable of the Spiritual Life

What does riding the river with Lewis and Clark have to do
with the Christian life? In this book it serves as a parable to help
illustrate two interrelated ideas:

- The triune God has a specific plan for your life journey;
- God the Father puts your life journey under the co-leadership of Jesus Christ and the Holy Spirit.

The Purpose and Limits of a Parable

A parable is a story designed to illustrate or teach a truth or religious principle. It takes something well known and compares it to something not so easy to grasp or understand. Jesus did much of His teaching through parables, communicating profound truths through the simplest of stories and metaphors.

While the stories of Jesus were about common human experiences, each story always pointed beyond itself to a spiritual meaning. When Jesus told a story about a farmer going out to sow seed (Matthew 13:3), or a manager making shrewd investments (Luke 16:1–9), His disciples knew that He was saying something about the Kingdom of God, or spiritual life. (If they did not get the point of one of His stories, they asked Him to explain it.)

A parable does not present an absolute match between the story and the idea being illustrated.[1] Some details of the story may be irrelevant to the message of the parable. Jesus told two parables to teach the importance of persevering in prayer. In one, He portrays God as a grouchy neighbor (Luke 11:5–13); in the other as an unjust judge (Luke 18:1–8). The point of the two parables is not to describe the character of God, but "to show [His disciples] that they should always pray and not give up" (Luke 18:1). The fact that God gets cast in unflattering roles does not detract from the value of these stories. A parable draws on certain parallels between a story and an idea being illustrated; it disregards details that do not contribute to the message.

The Lewis and Clark Story as a Parable

After reading about the Lewis and Clark Voyage of Discovery—in *Undaunted Courage*, the outstanding book by Stephen Ambrose, as well as in the words that both explorers wrote in their journals—I have come to share a deep regard for Meriwether

Lewis and William Clark. Their dedication to the task given them by President Jefferson, their leadership skills, and the general quality of their character evoke honest admiration. They are two authentic American heroes; they stand in the top rank of world explorers.

The journey of Lewis and Clark is a fascinating tale of exploration and discovery, the epic adventure of a young nation. Incidents that I recount in this book are accurate to the record, and often interesting in themselves. The events from the story threaded through the rest of this book, however, are not included merely as historical anecdotes. They are illustrations or metaphors of God's presence and guidance in our everyday life.

It is important to note that I do not present a historical appraisal of Lewis and Clark nor a detailed account of their journey. (For that, read *Undaunted Courage!*) I do not evaluate the significance of their exploration nor point out what might be seen as shortcomings or inconsistencies in their judgment. *My purpose is to select incidents from the story that illustrate the high adventure of knowing and following God's plan for your life.* When a Lewis and Clark incident comes up, you will immediately recognize that some aspect of this book's theme is being illustrated.

What particularly struck me in the Lewis and Clark story was the relationship between the two men. At the Lewis and Clark Festival in Great Falls, Montana, Stephen Ambrose spoke about this relationship. The effectiveness of their alliance—a sharing of command that disregarded military hierarchy—is unique to military history. Each was a strong individual and leader in his own right, yet the two men led the expedition with a unity that is a study for military historians to the present day. The journals give no hint of rivalry or conflict between them; according to Ambrose, "not so much as a cross word."[2]

President Thomas Jefferson, a "Third Presence"

Behind Lewis and Clark and the Corps of Discovery stood the figure of President Thomas Jefferson. His influence informed them like a third presence.[3] He had already secured himself a place in history with his authorship of the Declaration of Independence. Now he made his second great contribution to the development of America with the Louisiana Purchase. In one bold stroke of presidential leadership Jefferson doubled the size of the United States. He commissioned Lewis and Clark to explore this new part of the nation and report to him. The entire expedition took place against the backdrop of his presidential commission.

A Parable of the Trinity

In Jefferson, Lewis, and Clark we see *an extraordinary relationship*—two captains working in absolute harmony to carry out a highly specific commission given them by the president. They vividly illustrate how we may experience the Christian doctrine of the Trinity in everyday life.

The doctrine of the Trinity needs to come down off the bookshelf. It is more than an intellectual conversation piece; it gives direction to our experience of God's will in everyday life. The Bible was not given to satisfy human curiosity about obscure spiritual doctrines. It reveals, rather, what God considers necessary and helpful for life, our voyage of discovery: "The secret things belong to the Lord our God, but the things revealed belong to us and to our children forever, that we may follow all the words of this law" (Deuteronomy 29:29).

In the chapters that follow, we will consider how we may experience the presence and guidance of the three persons of the Trinity—Father, Son, and Holy Spirit—in everyday life. The relationship between Lewis and Clark and the father figure of President Thomas Jefferson serves as a parable, a recurring reminder that the plan for each of our lives is rooted in a relationship with the persons of the Holy Trinity. (See also appendix 1, "Extended Comment on the Doctrine of the Trinity.")

A Parable With a Specific Focus

The main point of our parable is the idea of a life journey[4] in which we experience divine leadership. The story of Jefferson,

Lewis, and Clark focuses on their relationships with one another and with the way they led the Corps of Discovery on a successful mission of exploration. Other events or aspects of their personal lives are not relevant to our purpose or to the symbolic roles that they fulfill in the parable.[5] Readers who find some aspect of the parable unhelpful may simply set it aside mentally. The basic theme of the book will stand without it.

Divine Guidance—a Lifelong Journey

"Following Jesus" or "being guided by the Holy Spirit" stands at the very center of the Christian life. Jesus' first words in calling His disciples were, "Follow Me." His words marked the beginning of a lifelong journey for them.

For the disciples, "divine guidance" was simply a matter of knowing Jesus, trusting Jesus, and following wherever He led them. Jesus taught them many things, but His teaching never displaced His personal leadership. Even after He left earth and returned to heaven, He promised to be with them. His personal leadership continued through His own spiritual presence and the presence of the Holy Spirit.

In chapter 6 we will look carefully at some of the ways God communicates with us. For this to make sense, we must consider the relationship on which it is based. This is the setting in which we will consider a biblical perspective for understanding and experiencing divine guidance: *a lifelong journey under the leadership of Jesus Christ and the Holy Spirit, according to the will and plan of God the Father.*

God has prepared a life plan for every person. When the apostle Paul took leave of the elders from Ephesus, he said to them, "I have not hesitated to proclaim to you the *whole will of God*" (Acts 20:27). The "whole will of God" that Paul proclaimed included the big picture. He told them about the plan of God for all people, "the mystery of Christ, which was not made known to men in other generations as it has now been revealed by the Spirit to God's holy apostles and prophets" (Ephesians 3:4–5).

The whole will of God also included a specific plan for each individual. "We are [God's] workmanship, created in Christ Jesus for good works, *which God prepared beforehand, that we should walk in them*" (Ephesians 2:10 RSV). God does not prepare a random selection of good works, then sit back and wait for volunteers. When God "prepares good works beforehand," He puts a name on them.

The message and calling that He sent to the village of Nazareth had a single name on it—Mary: "You have found favor with God. You will be with child and give birth to a son, and you are to give him the name of Jesus" (Luke 1:30–31).

God's plan for the first sweep of the gospel westward from Jerusalem, among Gentiles as well as Jews, had two names attached to it: "Set apart for me Barnabas and Saul for the work to which I have called them" (Acts 13:2).

In 1940, when England stood virtually alone against the towering might of the Nazi war machine, the nation turned to Winston Churchill for leadership. In his personal remembrance of that moment, Churchill wrote: "I cannot conceal from the reader of this truthful account that as I went to bed at about 3 A.M. I was conscious of a profound sense of relief. I felt as if I were walking with destiny, and that all my past life had been but a preparation for this hour and for this trial."[6] He recognized the calling that had fallen to him, and to England, in that dreaded hour. He summoned a staggered nation to lay life and all that was dear on the line in *the battle for Christian civilization*, which is how he repeatedly characterized World War II in his wartime speeches.

The Virgin Mary. Barnabas and the apostle Paul. Winston Churchill. Special people. Momentous events. But is a sense of divine purpose and destiny reserved only for the great and the famous? Or only for exceptional events?

In the chapters that follow, we will recount events from Scripture, and from experience, in which God leads quite ordinary people in quite ordinary happenings of their everyday lives. *At the outset, I share with you my conviction that God has prepared a life plan that has your name on it. It covers every aspect, age, and season of your life.*

God has provided a way for you to know and follow His plan for your life. Of course, the Christian life involves general truths that apply to all disciples. You can learn the truths, apply them with common sense, and experience a measure of God's leadership. But if that is all you do, your experience of divine guidance will fall short of what God has provided. Discerning God's will involves more than applying general truths with common sense, as Oswald Chambers points out with a touch of irony: "We put our common sense on the throne and then attach God's name to it."[7]

God's way of guiding you is more authentic and ultimately more reliable. He has planned a life journey in which a confident assurance of His presence becomes your everyday experience. This is no new or startling teaching. It is *normal Christianity*, according to the Bible. Yet it is often lacking in the experience of many Christians today.

My hope is that you will come to *a more frequent experience* of divine guidance in your own life. There is no experience more encouraging than to know that what you are doing is the will of God. This was the sustaining habit of Jesus' own life on earth: "My food . . . is to do the will of him who sent me" (John 4:34).

We pose the question to you and to ourselves: "How can I come to know God's will *more often*? How can I know, and follow, God's plan *every day of my life*?"

Jesus Christ and the Holy Spirit: Co-Commanders of Your Life Journey

The members of Lewis and Clark's Corps of Discovery were tough, knowledgeable frontiersmen. They brought various talents to the expedition, and they learned many things along the way. Yet none of them expected to make their way through an unexplored wilderness armed only with their own knowledge, training, and skill. Day by day they woke up to the same basic commitment: to follow where their captains would lead them.

The crowning reality of the Christian faith is the actual presence, in the life of a believer, of God the Father, of Jesus Christ, and of the Holy Spirit. In the chapters that follow we will consider some of the things we do in following God's plan for our lives. Our purpose is not simply to lay out spiritual principles to learn and put into practice, but also to consider more carefully how to maintain and deepen our relationship with the living God.

God's Leadership in Your Life Journey

There are no "Five Easy Steps to Discover God's Will for Your Life." Divine guidance cannot be reduced to a method or a spiritual formula. It is something that happens when the active leadership of your life is in the hands of the living God, the Holy Trinity.

On a scale of one to ten of "Things Important in My Spiritual Life," the doctrine of the Trinity scarcely makes a showing on the chart of many people. Yet this doctrine is at the heart of God's self-revelation. It is the Bible's way of describing who God is and what He does.

It is a huge tragedy that the doctrine of the Trinity has become the dusty haunt of theologians rather than a reality known and experienced by those following God's plan for their lives. In the early church, believers encountered the Holy Trinity—the heavenly Father, Jesus Christ the Son, and the Holy Spirit—as distinctive "persons." At the same time, they were gripped by the "Oneness" of God, the indivisible unity of Father, Son, and Holy Spirit.

Jesus spent the evening before His death going over this truth with His disciples: "If you love me, you will obey what I command. And I will ask the Father, and he will give you another Counselor to be with you forever—the Spirit of truth. . . . If anyone loves me, he will obey my teaching. My Father will love him, and we will come to him and make our home with him. . . . The

Counselor, the Holy Spirit, whom the Father will send in my name, will teach you all things and will remind you of everything I have said to you" (John 14:15–26).

In this book the truth of the Holy Trinity is presented not simply as a doctrine but as a practical key that can open our understanding, and our experience, of God's leadership in everyday life. Biblical principles and examples underscore a primary emphasis on *the indwelling presence and active leadership of the Holy Trinity in the life of a believer.*

The Lewis and Clark Expedition: An Epic Adventure

An Unexplored Wilderness

In 1800 America was a rambunctious teenager; the Constitution of the United States had been in effect just thirteen years. Two out of three Americans lived within fifty miles of the Atlantic Ocean. Only four roads crossed the Allegheny Mountains. A few frontier settlements were sprinkled from the Alleghenies to the Mississippi River, which was the western border of the United States.

West of the Mississippi lay an unexplored wilderness, already abounding with hopes and legends. For American settlers pressing ever westward, it presented the lure of plentiful land. Traders and speculators dreamed of discovering a "Northwest Passage," an all-water route from the Mississippi River to the Pacific Coast that would open a direct trade route to the Orient. Thomas Jefferson had fastened resolutely onto the dream of a Northwest Passage, and in 1800 he was elected the third president of the young nation.

Jefferson envisioned an empire stretching across the North American continent from the Atlantic to the Pacific. But other nations also had their eyes on this unexplored land of promise. In the seventeenth and eighteenth centuries, England, France, and

Spain had laid claim to huge tracts of land in North America, but for the most part they could not settle and govern these vast territories. Claims overlapped and caused wars, treaties, and contention.

In our life journey, the unexplored wilderness of Western America represents the undiscovered possibilities that lie before us in life.

The Louisiana Purchase

On July 4, 1803, a treaty was announced that changed the course of American history. It turned out to be one of the most important events in the history of the world. The *National Intelligencer*, a newspaper in Washington, D.C., reported that the government of the United States "has received official information that a Treaty was signed on the 30th of April, between the ministers of the United States and France, by which the United States has obtained full sovereignty over New Orleans, and the whole of Louisiana."

Two years earlier France's Napoleon had gained title to the Louisiana Territory in a treaty with Spain. "Louisiana" included the land northwest from New Orleans to the Rocky Mountains, then north to the headwaters of the Missouri River—a giant parallelogram of 820,000 square miles. In the power politics of that day, the claim did not mean much. A French army, even if it could run the gauntlet of British naval power and arrive in New Orleans, would be no match for a wave of robust American settlers spilling across the Mississippi River.

Napoleon made the shrewd decision to throw his weight on the side of the Americans. He was preparing for another war with England, and he needed money. When the Americans offered to buy New Orleans for two million dollars, he countered with an offer to sell the entire Louisiana Territory for fifteen million.

In a monumental act of presidential foresight and leadership, Thomas Jefferson seized the opportunity. He accepted the offer, doubling the size of the United States with a stroke of the pen.

Napoleon was jubilant with the deal. The sale, he said, would "strengthen forever" the power of the young United States. "I have just given England a rival who will sooner or later humble her pride."

Jefferson had already considered plans for an exploration of the Louisiana Territory and beyond, into what was known as the Oregon Country. The Oregon Country was a vague region subject to murky claims by half a dozen European nations and the United States, which had also laid claim when Robert Gray discovered the mouth of the Columbia River in 1795.

In his original plan for exploration, President Jefferson tried to assure foreign powers that any encroachment into their territory was in the disinterested spirit of expanding scientific and geographical knowledge. The Louisiana Purchase changed the situation. Now he could launch the expedition as an exploration of *American* territory. At least on paper, half of the West belonged officially to the United States, though no one knew for sure exactly what President Jefferson had bought.

In our life journey, the Louisiana Purchase represents the life of an individual person and God's claim upon that life.

The Leaders

Jefferson named Meriwether Lewis, together with another experienced military officer, William Clark, to head up an exploration of the Louisiana Purchase. Lewis came from the same part of Virginia as Jefferson, who knew his family and had known Lewis as a youth. When Jefferson, a widower, became president, he invited Lewis to become his personal secretary. Lewis lived with him like a son in the White House. Jefferson had absolute confidence that Lewis and Clark were the right ones to lead the expedition.

In our life journey, Jefferson, Lewis, and Clark represent divine leadership: the heavenly Father, Jesus Christ the Son, and the Holy Spirit.

A Clear Plan

On May 14, 1804, after months of preparation, Lewis and Clark entered the mouth of the Missouri River and headed upstream in command of the Corps of Discovery, a band of tough frontiersmen they had recruited for the exploration. Supplies for a journey that would last more than two years were crammed into three heavily laden boats.

Lewis and Clark's commission from President Jefferson was unmistakably clear: they were to explore the Missouri River in an attempt to discover the most direct and practical water route across the continent, for the purpose of commerce.

In our life journey, the commission of President Jefferson represents the life plan that God has for each person. Each one of us has a particular river to ride.

Into the Unexplored Territory, Day After Day

The first weeks of the journey were like a shakedown cruise. Captains and men got acquainted with one another, checked out equipment, and established procedures and discipline that would see them through the long journey.

In late September 1804, traveling through present-day South Dakota, they encountered a large band of the Teton Sioux Indians. President Jefferson's instructions were clear: "In all your intercourse with the natives treat them in the most friendly and conciliatory manner possible. Acquaint them with the peaceable dispositions of the United States, and of our wish to be neighborly, friendly, and useful to them."

The Teton Sioux were the terror of lesser Indian bands along the Missouri. They regularly extorted trade goods from hunters and trappers passing through their territory. Lewis and Clark, however, would not be scared or bluffed. Though outnumbered, they refused to pay tribute to the Teton warriors. Word of the confrontation spread across the prairie. As the Corps of Discovery proceeded north, other Indian tribes received them with a certain awe; captains who could humble the mighty Teton Sioux were deemed to have "strong medicine."

In the country of the Mandan Indians, near the present site of Bismarck, North Dakota, Lewis and Clark made winter camp

(1804–1805). Here they met the young Indian woman, Sacagawea, and her husband, Toussaint Charbonneau, a French trader. Between them, Sacagawea and Charbonneau understood a number of Indian dialects; Sacagawea was a member of the Shoshone tribe, through whose country the Corps of Discovery would pass the following spring.

When she was eleven years old, Sacagawea had been carried away from her Shoshone people by a raiding party of the Hidatsa tribe. Charbonneau won her in a bet with the warriors who had captured her. Later he married her. She was fifteen years old when Lewis and Clark first met her.

On April 7, 1805, the Corps of Discovery took leave of the friendly Mandans who had helped them survive a bitterly cold winter. They pushed their boats and canoes out into the Missouri, and once again began to pull upstream. Added to their company as interpreters were Sacagawea and Charbonneau, along with their infant son, just two months old.

In our life journey, the experiences, dangers, and adventures that the Corps of Discovery encountered along the way represent challenges, difficulties, opportunities, decisions, joys, and sorrows that we meet along the river of God's will for our life. The Indians that they met represent people or situations we encounter that play a role in God's plan for our life. Sacagawea and Charbonneau, like fellow members of the Corps of Discovery, represent people to whom we are more closely drawn, who share significantly in our life journey.

Challenges, Dangers, Hardships . . . and Final Victory

For the next four months the Corps of Discovery traveled through country of breathtaking beauty, teeming with game. Lewis wrote, "The country on both sides of the Missouri continues to be open, level, fertile, and beautiful as far as the eye can reach." They encountered herds of buffalo numbering in the tens of thousands. They had some encounters, and a few close scrapes, with grizzly bears. They managed an exhausting portage around the Great Falls of the Missouri. But in all this time they encountered not a single human being.

They continued to follow the Missouri on into the mountains. They came to the discouraging realization that a "Northwest Passage" was a pipe dream: there was no all-water route to the Pacific Ocean. The wide Missouri narrowed down to a stream that a man could step across.

The explorers expected to cross a single mountain range and then see the western slope before them. Instead they came on one mountain range after another. They had to abandon their canoes and find a way to cross the mountains. That meant horses. And that meant finding Indians to trade with.

On August 9 Lewis sighted the first person they had seen in this region, "an Indian on horseback about two miles distant coming down the plain toward us." His clothing was Shoshone. He was a young scout, all alone. As Lewis came closer, the Indian suddenly wheeled his horse and disappeared into the willow brush.

Lewis pressed on. Four days later they made contact with the main body of Shoshones. This was Sacagawea's home country; these were her people. The chief turned out to be her own brother. The Corps of Discovery spent the rest of the month among the Shoshones, trading for horses and preparing for a crossing of the mountains that the Indians called "The Bitterroots."

The crossing proved incredibly difficult. The way was steep, made worse by immense quantities of fallen timber. Several of the horses slipped and crashed down the hills. The horse carrying Clark's field desk rolled down the mountain for forty yards; the desk was smashed, but remarkably the horse was unhurt.

The crossing took more than half of September, with the men battling snow and treacherous terrain. They covered the last 160 miles in eleven days, one of the great forced marches in American history.

They proceeded down the Columbia River, meeting and trading with Indians along the way. On November 7, Clark wrote in his journal, "Great joy in the camp! We are in view of this great Pacific Ocean which we have been so long anxious to see."

Near the coast they built a winter camp. Clark named it Fort Clatsop, after the dominant Indian tribe in that area. Here the Corps of Discovery spent the wet and dreary winter of 1805–1806.

By early spring everyone was itching to begin the return journey. The party started back up the Columbia River on March 23, 1806. In the foothills of the Rocky Mountains they had to mark time for more than a month, waiting for the snows to melt. Then they crossed over to the eastern slope by a shorter, more direct route than they had followed in making the westward crossing. Two teenage boys from the Nez Percé tribe acted as their guides; in a superb feat of woodsmanship, the boys led them along a trail often buried under ten feet of snow.

On the return trip Lewis and Clark made further explorations and observations, according to their commission from President Jefferson.

Lewis and three of the party had a close brush with a small band of Blackfoot Indians, the most feared and warlike tribe on the northern plains, who tried to steal the guns and horses of the explorers. A shootout ensued. Lewis, bareheaded, felt the wind of a bullet whistle past his head. One of the Blackfoot braves was killed, another seriously injured. Lewis's presence of mind, coolness under fire, and a swift overnight march to rejoin the rest of the party prevented further incident. It was the lone outbreak of hostilities between the Corps of Discovery and any of the Indians that they met during the entire journey. Jefferson's instructions—to meet the Indian inhabitants in the most friendly manner possible—proved counsel of uncommon wisdom.

In Mandan country they took leave of Sacagawea, Charbonneau, and young "Pomp," the nickname the men had given to Sacagawea's baby boy. Upon their departure, Clark wrote in a letter to Charbonneau, "Your woman, who accompanied you that long, dangerous and fatiguing route to the Pacific Ocean and back, deserved a greater reward for her services than we had in our power to give her."

Two years earlier, the Corps of Discovery had started up the Missouri, paddling against the current, sometimes gaining as little as two or three miles a day—more a collection of hardy, adventurous men than a disciplined Corps. They returned with the current at their back, frequently covering up to seventy miles a day. Stephen Ambrose describes their triumphal return to St. Louis on September 23, 1806: Lewis and Clark "had taken thirty-odd unruly soldiers and molded them into the Corps of Discovery, an elite platoon of tough, hardy, resourceful, well-disciplined men. They had earned the men's absolute trust. They had completed the epic voyage."[8]

A Long Journey

Before Lewis and Clark launched their expedition, there had been considerable talk about exploring the Louisiana Territory, and even a few attempts, but none successful. Lewis and Clark turned talk and speculation into a victorious experience. Their expedition replaced the "pipe dream" of a Northwest Passage with firsthand knowledge of the vast new territory that had been added to the United States.

A Parable With a Distinctive Focus

During their epic journey, the needs of individual members of the Corps of Discovery were provided for. Obtaining food, water, and safe campsites was a daily necessity. The captains measured with care when the men needed rest. "Stopped to refresh the men, who suffered very much from the heat," wrote Clark on a steamy July afternoon early in the journey.

Mere personal comfort, however, scarcely had a place in the vocabulary of the Corps of Discovery. "The current excessively rapid and difficult to ascend," wrote Lewis the following summer, when they approached the Great Falls of the Missouri, "great numbers of dangerous places, and the fatigue which we have to encounter is incredible; the men in the water from morning until night, hauling the boats with cords, walking on sharp rocks and over slippery stones which alternately cut their feet and throw them down; notwithstanding all this difficulty they go with great cheerfulness; added to those difficulties, the rattle snakes are innumerable and require great caution to prevent being bitten."

In much of contemporary Christianity the focus has locked in on people and their needs. Churches are encouraged to be user-friendly: "Tell us your needs. Bring us your problems. Let us show you how God can bless you."

Having one's immediate needs taken care of, however, is not the primary focus of Christian discipleship. Jesus said, "If anyone would come after me [become my disciple], he must deny himself and take up his cross and follow me" (Matthew 16:24). When Jesus took up His cross, He followed His Father's will, unto death.

Under the leadership of Lewis and Clark, personal needs and concerns never detracted from the primary focus of the expedition, which was to complete the journey assigned by President Jefferson. In the summer of 1805, Clark wrote, "All [in the Corps of Discovery] appear perfectly to have made up their minds to succeed in the expedition *or perish in the attempt*. We all believe that we are about to enter on the most perilous and difficult part of our Voyage, yet I see no one repining; all appear ready to meet those difficulties which await us with resolution and admirable fortitude."

Similarly, you are to discover—and to follow with determination—the plan that God has set out for your life: to become the person He has created you to become and to do what He calls you to do.[9] Personal needs and problems find their place in relation to this central purpose.

"We proceeded on."

In recent years, many people have experienced spiritual renewal in such settings as the Billy Graham crusades, Campus Crusade for Christ, charismatic communities, youth movements, the "Jesus People" revival, small groups, prayer fellowships, and Bible studies. The renewal has been genuine, often life-transforming. But after beginning, many find it difficult to continue. The dynamic ebbs away. The power or will to press on grows weak. What can keep the hope alive? How does a vision get translated into reality?

One unremarkable phrase, recurring over and over in the Lewis and Clark journals, tells perhaps as well as anything why the Voyage of Discovery succeeded: *"We proceeded on."*

People who embark on the adventure of knowing and following God's plan for their lives need encouragement to proceed on! It is my hope that this book will prove helpful to you in your own voyage of discovery, that the presence and power and guidance of the living God may become not only talk but a more consistent happening in your everyday life—a victorious experience as you Ride the River of God's empowering presence.

CHAPTER TWO

THE PLAN

God has a specific plan for your life journey.

THE LOUISIANA PURCHASE opened the possibility for the fulfill-ment of Thomas Jefferson's vision—an American empire stretch-ing from the Atlantic to the Pacific. In 1803, this grand vision included few details. West of the Mississippi River lay an unex-plored wilderness. The Lewis and Clark expedition would map this wilderness and incorporate it into the American nation.

By Jefferson's command they were to follow the Missouri River to its headwaters, portage across to the Columbia River or one of its tributaries, and follow that river to its mouth on the Pacific Ocean. Their commission was plain, unmistakable: *they were to go to a known destination by a certain, but as yet uncharted, way.*

A Voyage of Discovery

The Christian life, from beginning to end, is a voyage of dis-covery.

- *The destination is known:* the Bible calls it the Kingdom of Heaven, or eternal life;
- *The route is certain:* it is the "river of God's will," the life plan that God has for you;
- *The way is not yet charted:* every day you push forward into the unexplored territory of God's plan for your life.

In this life journey, God does not intend divine guidance to be the now-and-then thing that many Christians accept as normal—occasional episodes when we find ourselves in a quandary, hoping that God will tell us what to do. Divine guidance is meant to be the day-by-day experience of those who live out the plan of God the Father, under the leadership of Jesus Christ and the Holy Spirit.

The Lewis and Clark expedition was the practical venture that incorporated the Louisiana Purchase into the United States. The apostle Paul reminds us that our life has been purchased by God: "You are not your own; you were bought at a price" (1 Corinthians 6:19–20). Your life, from birth to death, is a voyage of discovery to find out what kind of a "purchase" the Lord has in you. As Jefferson purchased land for the American nation, God the Father purchased our lives for His Kingdom.

> Blessed assurance, Jesus is mine!
> O what a foretaste of glory divine!
> Heir of salvation, *purchase of God*,
> Born of His Spirit, washed in His blood.

Every person has a river to ride. The basic direction is clear at the outset. God has laid out a plan for your life, a river that you are to follow. You are like a person who has signed on with the Corps of Discovery.

The Bible, history, other people, and common sense can tell you some of the things you are likely to encounter. But you will discover the actual plan for your life only as you make the journey.

If you were your own boss, you could strike out in any number of directions, but not when you are in God's Corps of Discovery. God's command is plain, and it covers your life from beginning to end: you are to Ride the River.

God's plan for your life is specific. To Ride the River describes a life on its way to being incorporated into what the Bible calls the Kingdom of Heaven. It is a life committed to knowing and following the plan of God; a life of one who "does not live his earthly life for selfish human desires, but rather *for the will of God*" (1 Peter 4:2).

If someone were to ask, "What is your purpose in life?" you might answer, "To do the will of God." That would be a good, all-encompassing answer to the question of What? but it would leave hanging in the air the question of How?

When you Ride the River, your understanding of the will of God must move beyond generalities; it must become specific to your personal life. In Scripture, God has revealed His basic plan for mankind[1] in some detail. What He has *not* revealed in detail is the strategy for working out His plan in *your life*.

When Saul of Tarsus had a vision of the risen Lord Jesus Christ on the road to Damascus, he asked, "What shall I do, Lord?" The Lord said, "Go into Damascus. There you will be told all that you have been assigned to do." In Damascus, a believer named Ananias came to him and said, "The God of our fathers has chosen you to know His will and to see the Righteous One and to hear words from his mouth. You will be his witness to all men of what you have seen and heard" (Acts 22:10, 14–15). God's plan for Saul of Tarsus (later to become the apostle Paul) involved more than a general call to help spread the message concerning Jesus. God had a life plan for him that was individual, specific. It began with a simple command from the Risen Christ. It continued throughout the rest of Paul's life under the leadership of Jesus Christ and the Holy Spirit.

If living according to the will of God means applying scriptural truth with common sense—*that and nothing more*—we are like kids who get together at the local park to play football. We choose up sides and immediately launch into a game, improvising as we go. The idea of having a coach who drills us on the fundamentals of the game, who has a well-planned strategy that will lead to victory on a real football field, is beyond our experience.

God's will rests upon fundamentals revealed in Scripture. We must learn these and apply them in everyday life. But His will also includes a divine strategy for achieving the life plan He has set for you as an individual. His *will* is wedded to His *way*. The key to finding His way is not a formula or a method that we learn. It is embedded in a *relationship*. Jesus pointed to it when He said, "*I* am the way and the truth and the life" (John 14:6).

Your life belongs to God. He purchased it. When your life is lived according to God's will, it is incorporated into God's Kingdom. This does not mean machinelike submission to the decrees of a powerful Potentate, but a day-by-day relationship with the God-appointed leaders for your life journey.

This calls to mind the solemn and cheerful awareness of the men in the Corps of Discovery. They knew from the beginning that the plan was to follow the river *under the command of Lewis and Clark*. It was the adventure of a lifetime, and they eagerly stood in line to sign up.

In the Lord's Prayer, Jesus taught His disciples to focus first on the name, the kingdom, and the will of the Father. When you observe these priorities, everything else falls into place, including your personal life plan.

This is the lifestyle that Jesus himself modeled in the presence of His disciples. He was not guided simply by general principles and reason. He was above all else the Son of His Father in Heaven. He said, "When you have lifted up the Son of Man, then you will know that I am the one I claim to be, and that I do nothing on my own but speak just what the Father has taught me. I tell you the truth, the Son can do nothing by himself; He can do only what He sees His Father doing, because whatever the Father does the Son also does" (John 8:28, 5:19). Jesus lived in the empowering presence of the heavenly Father. His lifestyle was rooted in that relationship, expressing itself in obedience and accountability in order to accomplish the purpose for which the Father had sent Him.

We do not wander around in the unexplored territory of our life to find our fortune, to "fulfill ourselves," to make our own plans, to gratify our own desires. We do not strike off on our own in search of gold or hidden treasure. We do not chase after success, or convenience, or comfort, or pleasure, or status according to some worldly standard. We do not wander aimlessly. We do not give up when the going gets tough. God's plan is simple and straightforward, and it covers our life from beginning to end: we Ride the River. We follow our divine Co-Captains, the Lord Jesus Christ and the Holy Spirit, because we are a purchase of God.

The Corps of Discovery Has CLEAR DIRECTION

Ride the River means that your life has purpose and clear direction. God has a specific plan for your life. You can know it and follow it.

This idea is still strange to many Christians. They believe that we can know God's will in terms of general do's and don'ts. They think it presumptuous to say we can know God's will in specific matters that come up in everyday life. They are like members of the Corps of Discovery heading upriver without Lewis and Clark. In this topsy-turvy scenario, people do not expect Jesus Christ and the Holy Spirit to lead but to trail along afterward and "bless what we have done."

God has no plan for us to Ride the River under our own leadership. In the following chapters we will consider how the leadership of Jesus Christ and the Holy Spirit can become a practical reality in our everyday life. We will look carefully at the biblical evidence. God has provided no other arrangement for our life as Christians. When you Ride the River, the presence and leadership of Jesus Christ and the Holy Spirit are essential.

Society pumps up young people, saying, "You can be anything you want to be!" Conventional wisdom encourages them to formulate goals for their life: "Where do you want to be five years from now? Ten years from now?" The implication, throughout our culture, is that the direction of our life is up to us.

In God's Corps of Discovery, a different mentality prevails.

"Where will I be ten years from now *if I Ride the River?* Where will our family, our congregation, our friendship be *if we Ride the River?*" The question is not what I want to do with my life, but what has God planned for my life. The focus is first on discernment, only then on decision. The decision is always to follow where the Lord leads.

When my father, Ade Christenson, graduated from college, he planned to go to medical school. One afternoon he was sitting on his front porch when a man who had graduated a couple of years ahead of him came walking up the street. They started talking. The man was on his way to the college placement office to inform them that he was leaving a coaching job at a small high school in Iowa: the position would be open.

"Why don't you take the job?" he said to my father. "You were active in sports, the Honor Athlete of your class. In a year or two you could save up money for medical school."

My father applied for the job . . . and stayed in coaching the rest of his life. When he died at 93, Jim Klobuchar, one of his former athletes, then a newspaper columnist for the *Minneapolis Star Tribune*, wrote: "He came to my hometown for one year as the high school coach in the middle of World War II when the college where he coached had temporarily discontinued football. He was directly involved in my life for two months, 49 years ago. Yet apart from my father, I know of only two or three men who revealed more to me in all the years that went before or after."[2]

After his retirement, my father said to me, "I didn't realize it at the time, but I believe God put me out on the front porch that day. I was supposed to be a coach."

You can probably look back on some aspect of your own life and say something similar. God's plan for your life is far more in His hands than in yours. That doesn't mean that we might just as well sit back and let things happen. God wants the eyes of our heart to be enlightened in order that we may know what is the hope to which He has called us. But God does not wait around doing nothing until we come knocking at His door, asking for guidance. He plans and directs our lives according to the counsel of His will. (Ephesians 1:18, 5) Our awareness of His direction, or a fuller understanding of it, may come later.

Discussions of divine guidance often focus too quickly on what we must do to get an answer. But guidance is more rooted in relationship than in spiritual methodology. The kind of answer we get depends upon the kind of question with which we begin. Members of God's Corps of Discovery are concerned about God's guidance when they have a decision to make, but they have a different point of beginning than is common in our individualistic culture. They begin with the questions, "What does *God* have in mind here? Where does *His* will lead?" They do not simply strike out in a direction that looks interesting or promising to them. They Ride the River.

Speaking at a meeting of the Association of American Physicians and Surgeons, Dr. Ed Payne, a specialist in family medicine, said: "The crisis of American medicine is not tobacco, AIDS, silicone, the Gulf War Syndrome, breast or any other form of cancer, physician-assisted suicide, euthanasia, licensure, medical care for the poor, or any other specific medical or ethical issue. The crisis of American medicine is far greater than any one of these problems; indeed, it is far greater than all of them combined, because the answers to these problems do not come from within them, but from medical ethics. It is the same crisis that faces our culture in every other area: How do we decide what is right and what is wrong? Is there a method which will stand the test of time, or do ethics change with changing cultures? How are medical-ethical decisions made today?"[3]

Dr. Payne poses a serious question that doctors face, but at its root is a question we all face. How is *any* decision made today? This is the kind of down-to-earth question that this book addresses—not handing out answers, but pointing to a relationship with the triune God that leads us to know His will in concrete situations.

Life choices for members of the Corps of Discovery are SPE-CIFIC. Before the Voyage of Discovery got under way, Lewis flirted with the idea of making a preliminary exploration toward the Southwest, where the Spanish had found gold and silver. President Jefferson wrote him a stern letter, reminding him of the plan to ride the Missouri River to its headwaters. From that point on, neither Lewis nor Clark, nor any member of the Corps of Discovery, ever questioned the president's specific commission: they would follow the river.

Seen from the outside, as a group, Christians enjoy a broad range of choices. At the individual level, however, the life choices of a Christian disciple are limited. They are tied to the specific will of God.

Each person has a particular river to ride. The Lord creates a different life plan for each individual, even for those whose lives may be closely related to one another. Each person has a specific task and calling, related to his or her talents and abilities, and perhaps to other considerations that only the Lord knows about.

At a national pastors conference that his congregation sponsors annually, Don Meares, pastor of a large multiracial church in the Washington, D.C., area, said, "If God's plan for you was to go into business, and you decided to become a minister, you missed God's will, big time!"

William Bennett vividly captures the varieties of Christian service with the retelling of an old legend, one of the selections he included in *The Moral Compass*: "The old monk saw how many ways there are of serving God. Some serve Him in churches and hermits' cells by praise and prayer. Some serve Him on the highway, helping strangers in desperate need. Some live faithfully and gently in humble homes, working, bringing up children, remaining kind and cheerful. Some bear pain patiently, for His sake. Endless, endless ways there are, that only the Heavenly Father sees."[4]

I think of the gift of hospitality shown by many families in our congregation, opening their homes to groups and individuals over many years. The spiritual revival in our congregation was sparked in a prayer group, sitting in a circle in front of the fireplace in the home of Bob and Greta Scott in 1960. For many years the young people in our congregation descended on the home of Bud and Jean Hahn or Bob and Greta Scott for Friday night volleyball. When I travel overseas, I have had people tell me, sometimes as many as thirty years later, that their stay with one of the families in our congregation marked a spiritual milestone in their lives.

The life of a believer—of a family, a congregation, a community committed to the will of God—is narrow, not in a legalistic sense, but in a *strategic* sense. God's will embraces not only His moral law and His plan of salvation in a general sense, but also His plan for your personal life journey. If you Ride the River, many choices will be ruled out, not because they are wrong in themselves but because they head away from the particular river that God has given you to follow. No decision, however ordinary, is unimportant if it advances you along the river that God has set before you.

Al Olguin and his wife, Halldis, had six children. Al was a jolly man with an infectious sense of humor. One of his sons came begging for a new skateboard: "All the kids in the neighborhood have new skateboards!" the child chanted.

"No they don't," Al replied, tousling his son's hair. "*You* don't!"

He related this in speaking about a decision he and Halldis had made to live within their income. The family budget didn't have room for a new skateboard that month. Following through on the will of God touches the normal happenings of everyday life.

When Jesus called His disciples, He usually said simply, "Follow Me." He did not immediately explain what this would involve. Yet His call narrowed the basic direction of their life down to one specific goal: as individuals, they would follow where Jesus led.

The life of present-day disciples has the same specific focus. It goes beyond simply living by certain biblical principles. It looks and listens for God to reveal His specific direction. "Your ears shall hear a word behind you, saying, 'This is the way, walk in it,' Whenever you turn to the right hand or whenever you turn to the left" (Isaiah 30:21 NKJV). Riding the River of God's will calls for a lively expectation that God has not gone silent. He still speaks to people, though in ways that we must patiently learn. It calls for a mind-set well characterized by Luthor Nelson, the youth worker in our congregation, as "premeditated obedience."[5] This is the hallmark of the Spirit-filled life: God gives the Holy Spirit to those who obey Him (Acts 5:32). Every bend in the River can reveal new, unexpected challenges. Occasional obedience is not adequate to the task. We must decide beforehand that we will obey God's leading.

The leadership of Jesus Christ and the Holy Spirit is anything but stereotyped. It does not follow a set formula. We need to resist the natural tendency to reduce the Christian life to a method, rather than depending on the present leading of the Holy Spirit. The apostle Paul warned the Galatians about this danger: "After beginning with the Spirit, are you now trying to attain your goal by human effort?" (Galatians 3:3). Maybe for a month you went without lunch, perhaps to pray about something at work. The Lord walked you through that situation. His presence and guidance were real. Now something else comes up, and the thought pops into your mind, "I'll give up lunch and pray about it." That *may* be the leading of the Spirit, but He might have a different plan this time. It is well to remember that God does not endorse human methods that displace the present leadership of Jesus Christ and the Holy Spirit.

Another caution: When you Ride the River, you must steer clear of the temptation to turn the Lord's word to you into a law or obligation for other people. Jesus once made it clear to Peter that a particular word was meant for him, not necessarily for others:

> Jesus said [to Peter], "When you were younger you dressed yourself and went where you wanted; but when you

are old you will stretch out your hands, and someone else will dress you and lead you where you do not want to go." Jesus said this to indicate the kind of death by which Peter would glorify God. Then he said to him, "Follow Me!" Peter turned and saw that the disciple whom Jesus loved was following them [and] asked, "Lord, what about him?" Jesus answered, "If I want him to remain alive until I return, what is that to you. You must follow me" (John 21:18–22).

"Follow Me" is the refrain that accompanies every step of our life journey as Christians. More than anything else, it turns a staid religion of duty into the adventure of a lifetime.

Riding the River is HARD WORK!

Riding the River requires discipline, courage, and persistence. It is no accident that the Bible speaks often of the need for endurance. The temptation is always at hand to stop, build a cabin by the riverside, and settle down, rather than follow the river to its headwaters.

How do we overcome this temptation? More than anything, it depends upon the *presence and leadership of our divine Captains.* Our own resolve and good intentions might get us partway up the river. For the expedition to fully succeed, the Captains must be in charge.

CHAPTER THREE

THE PARTNERSHIP

*God's plan for the Christian life is that we live it out under the
active, hands-on leadership of Jesus Christ and the Holy Spirit.*

LEWIS AND CLARK have become a byword in American history.
Like "salt and pepper," you seldom say one without the other. Virtually from the moment President Jefferson first spoke to Meriwether Lewis about exploring the Louisiana Territory, Lewis
sensed that the success of the venture depended upon a partnership
with William Clark. When they met and shook hands in Clarks-
ville in the Indiana Territory on the way to St. Louis, the Voyage
of Discovery was officially underway.

A Partnership that is CLOSE and PERSONAL

Christians in the New Testament were led by the divine partnership of Jesus Christ and the Holy Spirit. Jesus himself prepared
His disciples to receive the Holy Spirit as Co-Commander of the
journey that lay ahead of them. The Holy Spirit "will teach you
all things, and will remind you of everything I have said to
you.... You know Him, for He lives with you and will be in
you" (John 14:26, 17). The divine Captains directed the day-by-
day lives of believers, according to the plan of God the Father. The
leadership of the living God was close.

As Christians today, we need to be on guard that the forceful
experience of the early church does not shrivel into a historical

memory or a lifeless system of intellectual beliefs. That would be like members of the Corps of Discovery heading upriver with nothing more than anecdotes and lecture notes from Lewis and Clark. In the day-to-day business of riding the river, their captains would be a memory rather than a presence.

God's plan for the Christian life has always been that it be lived out under the active, hands-on leadership of Jesus Christ and the Holy Spirit. Part of the purpose of this book is to revisit certain Scriptures and doctrines of the Christian faith that show this, and ask, "How can this become a reality in our everyday experience?"

The scriptural evidence is unmistakable. The Bible says that God himself shall indwell believers. The apostle Paul recites this truth in a moving rhapsody of praise:

> I bow my knees before the Father, from whom every family in heaven and on earth is named, that according to the riches of his glory he may grant you to be strengthened with might *through his Spirit in the inner man*, and that *Christ may dwell in your hearts through faith*; that you, being rooted and grounded in love, may have the power to comprehend with all the saints what is the breadth and length and height and depth, and to know the love of Christ which surpasses knowledge, *that you may be filled with all the fullness of God.*
>
> Now to him who *by the power at work within us* is able to do far more abundantly than all that we ask or think, to him be glory in the church and in Christ Jesus to all generations, for ever and ever. Amen. (Ephesians 3:14–21 RSV)

This is an amazing revelation. The Apostle prays that God, in all His fullness, shall indwell the lives of these believers. But what does this phrase mean—*the fullness of God?*

God—a "Divine Family"

God has a life in himself that is family-like. Human families, says the Apostle, are an echo of the family life of God.

During a theological consultation in the mid–1970s, Lutheran theologian Warren Quanbeck observed that the church, when it wrote the early creeds, used categories of Greek philosophy. The Nicene Creed, for example, describes Jesus as "being of one *substance* with the Father." ("Substance" was a category in Greek philosophy.) These categories, Quanbeck said, may not be useful for communicating with people today; we may need to use other expressions. Asked what kind of expression he might suggest, Quanbeck responded, "Perhaps a category like *family* would be more useful in our day."[1]

The category of family takes us back to the creation story. God said, " 'Let Us make man in Our image, according to Our likeness. . . . ' So God created man in His own image; in the image of God He created him; male and female He created them" (Genesis 1:26–27 NKJV).

This is the Bible's first description of human beings. They were created "in the image of God." The way the Bible presents this truth suggests a unique community concept of God. "Then *God* [grammatically plural, yet decisively singular in meaning] said, 'Let *Us* [plural] make *man* [singular] in *Our* [plural] image.' " From the days of the early church, Bible scholars have interpreted this curious intertwining of singular and plural as pointing to the Holy Trinity: one God, yet a community of persons.[2]

At this all-important beginning point, when God creates man, Scripture highlights a particular aspect of man's nature, namely, that which corresponds to the family-like aspect of God's nature: God creates man *as male and female*—not a solitary individual, but two distinct persons, who nevertheless "become one" (see Genesis 2:24, 5:1–2, Ephesians 5:28). *When God wanted to put something on earth that was uniquely like himself, He created a community, a human family.*[3]

The Bible reveals that God is diverse (three persons), yet unmistakably One. It would be hard to find a metaphor that so effortlessly brings together the concepts of unity and diversity as the common human experience of family.

When my mother lay dying at the age of 93, she spoke succinctly and simply about her prayer life: "Sometimes I pray to the Father, when it's something big, like for the nation or the church. When it's personal, I pray to Jesus. When it's for others—when we need something *done!*—I call on the Holy Spirit."

"That's something like a family," I said. "In one situation a child talks with his father, another time with his mother, sometimes with a brother or sister."

"Yes, but it's all family talk," she said, smiling. "Sometimes you and your brother tried to play your father and me off against each other, but it never worked. We stuck together."

Two months later she died, looking forward to seeing her God, and the husband she had lived with for nearly seventy years. They were two distinct, colorful, and decidedly different individuals, yet when either of them spoke a decision, we children knew that we had heard the other as well. In will and purpose, they were one.

To be indwelt by the fullness of God means that the divine family—the heavenly Father, Jesus Christ the Son, and the Holy Spirit—dwells in us, according to the eternal wisdom and purpose of the Father. The Bible is unmistakably clear: God in all His fullness, *but also in all the distinctiveness of His triune identity*, will indwell the lives of believers.

God means to share His life with us in the fullest and most intimate way possible. Disciples will experience:

- the indwelling power of the Spirit;
- the indwelling love of Christ;
- finally, the indwelling presence of "all the fullness of God."

This brings the doctrine of the Trinity off the bookshelf and into the lives and experiences of men and women in everyday life.

A Partnership that is PRESENT and ACTIVE

The Heavenly Father, Present and Active

Jesus told His disciples that the God whom they addressed in prayer as "Our Father in Heaven . . ." would also be a Presence in their earthly lives. "If anyone loves me, he will obey my teaching. My Father will love him, and we will come to him and make our home with him" (John 14:23). Jesus prayed that the disciples would share an intimacy with the Father that He himself enjoyed: "Father, just as you are in me and I am in you, may they also be in us. . . . I in them and you in me . . . that the love you have for me may be in them, and that I myself may be in them" (John 17:21–23, 26).

Jesus Christ, Present and Active

Jesus promised to return and be present with His disciples following His ascension to heaven: "Make disciples of all nations, baptizing them in the name of the Father and of the Son and of the Holy Spirit, teaching them to observe all things that I have commanded you; and lo, *I am with you always*, even to the end of the age" (Matthew 28:19–20 NKJV).[4]

The apostle Paul experienced and taught the indwelling presence of Jesus Christ as a pivotal mystery of the faith: "I have been crucified with Christ and I no longer live, but *Christ lives in me*" (Galatians 2:20).[5]

In the New Testament, after Jesus ascended back to heaven, people continued to experience His presence as an unmistakable reality. For example, "They tried to enter Bithynia, but *the Spirit of Jesus* would not allow them to" (Acts 16:7).[6]

To be divinely guided means that Christ's indwelling presence becomes an increasingly conscious reality in your everyday life. But there is more . . .

The Holy Spirit, Present and Active

In addition to His own continuing presence, Jesus promised that He would send another Counselor to His disciples. The Counselor would be like himself, yet not identical to himself. "The world cannot accept [the Spirit of truth], because it neither sees him nor knows him. But you know him, for *he lives with you and will be in you*" (John 14:17).[7]

From the Day of Pentecost onward, the early church knew the presence and power of the Holy Spirit—not simply as a theological doctrine but as an indwelling presence, a person whom they experienced in their everyday life, time and time again. "After they prayed, the place where they were meeting was shaken. And they were all *filled with the Holy Spirit* and spoke the word of God boldly" (Acts 4:31).[8]

Hands-on Leadership

Members of the Corps of Discovery could not depend simply on instruction, on maps and notes, or on their past experience when they rode the river. The expedition thrust them into unforeseen situations almost every day. They needed the competent, hands-on leadership of Lewis and Clark to accomplish the plan laid out by President Jefferson.

Sometimes this leadership spelled the difference between life and death. Once a group exploring along the bank of the Missouri was overtaken by a flash flood. Clark saw it coming. He scrambled up the hill pushing Sacagawea and her child before him, barely escaping a torrent of water fifteen feet high.

Clark's rescue of Sacagawea and her infant son was typical of the leadership the captains exercised throughout the expedition. The evident commitment of Lewis and Clark to the commission entrusted to them by President Jefferson meant unreserved commitment to every member of the Corps of Discovery.

Riding the River is serious business. Our destiny in this life, and in the next, is at stake. The Father does not want or expect us to muddle through on our own. Nor does He want us to launch out knowing one Captain but not the other. His plan calls for the hands-on leadership of Jesus Christ and the Holy Spirit.

You cannot read far into the story of Jesus without discovering a man of absolute commitment, a commitment with a single focus. When He called His first disciples with the words, "Come, follow me" (Matthew 4:19), He could easily have added, "as I follow the Father." He modeled a life totally dedicated to knowing and following the heavenly Father's will.

Once, when critics challenged Him to prove that His teaching was from God, Jesus said, "When you have lifted up the Son of Man, then you will know that I am the one I claim to be, and that *I do nothing on my own but speak just what the Father has taught me*" (John 8:28). On the night before His death, Jesus said to His disciples, "If anyone loves me, he will obey my teaching. My Father will love him, and we will come to him and make our home with him. He who does not love me will not obey my teaching. *These words you hear are not my own; they belong to the Father who sent me*" (John 14:23–24).

Everything He did answered to a single motive: "I tell you the truth, the Son can do nothing by himself; He can do only what He sees His Father doing, because whatever the Father does the Son also does" (John 5:19).

Jesus was in continual communication with the Father. What the Father said and did in heaven, Jesus said and did on earth. It was the unvarying example of His life.

When He told His disciples about the coming of the Holy Spirit, they saw that this "other Counselor" would be no different. But now there would be an added dimension: they, too, would learn what the Father was saying and doing. "When he, the Spirit of truth, comes, he will guide you into all truth. He will not speak on his own; he will speak only what he hears, and he will tell you what is yet to come. He will bring glory to me by taking from what is mine and making it known to you. All that belongs to the Father is mine. That is why I said the Spirit will take from what is mine and make it known to you" (John 16:13–15).

When we receive the Holy Spirit, He brings into our lives a determination to work in us the same devotion to the will of the Father that is present in Jesus and in himself.

Charles Sheldon's bestselling novel *In His Steps* depicted a community that resolved to live according to the question, "What would Jesus do?"[9] Recently a movement among Christians picked up on the theme. Kids and adults all over the country could be seen with T-shirts, caps, pencils, coffee mugs, and wristlets with the acrostic, WWJD.

If we look at the WWJD question from a biblical point of view, it involves more than simply imitating the example of Jesus by doing what is "right." Jesus certainly lived according to the commandments of God. He was, by any measure, a "good man." But God's will for His life involved more than simply keeping the commandments. He had a particular river to ride.

One day He rounded a sharp bend in the river. Dead ahead lay a treacherous stretch of rapids with a drop-off in clear sight—in the shape of a Roman cross. Jesus sensed that the Father's plan for His life went straight over the falls. Some in the party shouted in protest, "Never, Lord! This shall never happen to you!" (Matthew 16:22).

Jesus paddled out into midstream; He would ride this stretch of river alone. Jesus was more than a "good" man—He was *God's* man. The single best key to understanding His life and calling is the word He spoke to His disciples: "My food is to do the will of him who sent me and to finish his work" (John 4:34).

Every person committed to knowing and following God's plan in everyday life has this encouragement: it is the life that Jesus himself lived; it is the life He promises to His followers through the leadership that He and the Holy Spirit bring into their lives.

Theoretically, God could have planned for the Christian life to be directed simply by good teaching, well learned and earnestly followed. Some people labor under the mistaken belief that He actually did this, once the final book of the Bible had been written (around A.D. 100).

Or, God could have left everything up to the leadership of Jesus Christ alone. Some evangelical teaching may provoke this misconception. Like the bureaucrats in the War Department who were reluctant to assign Clark an equal rank with Lewis, they presume to elevate Christ by downplaying the Holy Spirit.[10] Such thinking is out of touch with the mind of Christ. Jesus does not countenance any downgrading of the Co-Commander whom the Father has sent.

At the other extreme, some Pentecostal or charismatic teaching may so emphasize the empowering work of the Holy Spirit that the active co-leadership of Jesus Christ suffers neglect.

These misconceptions go against the plain meaning of the Scriptures that you have just read. The Bible reveals the Father's plan with unmistakable clarity: Your voyage of discovery—the God-created plan for your life journey—is meant to proceed under the active co-command of Jesus Christ and the Holy Spirit.

A Partnership that WORKS!

Lewis and Clark each had distinctive gifts that they contributed to the Voyage of Discovery. Lewis was more the scientist and philosopher. He often walked along the land lying near the river, observing and recording the plant and animal life as President Jefferson had requested. This left Clark on the river, more involved with the everyday leading, training, and discipline of the men.

In their relationship with each other, Lewis and Clark were remarkably unassertive. They seemed to have an unspoken agreement about the ways and the places in which each would exercise leadership. References to one another in their journals are couched in terms of uncommon respect. When the Corps of Discovery divided into two exploring parties for a short time, Lewis wrote, "I took leave of my worthy friend and companion, Captain Clark, and the party that accompanied him. I could not avoid feeling much concern on this occasion although I hoped the separation was only momentary." Reporting on Lewis's recovery from a hunting accident near the end of the journey, Clark wrote, "I am happy to find that my worthy friend, Captain Lewis, is so well as to walk about with ease."[11] The word of the apostle Paul, "Outdo one another in showing honor" (Romans 12:10 RSV), could have been written about Lewis and Clark's personal relationship. The way that they led the expedition was complementary, not competitive.[12] They took it for granted, as did their subordinates, that both leaders were commissioned and were necessary to carry out the plan of President Jefferson.

Members of the Corps of Discovery related to Lewis and Clark in a natural, pragmatic way. On occasion Lewis would assign a contingent of the Corps to a particular task; in another situation Clark would lead. According to a command or undertaking that came their way, members of the Corps of Discovery would follow the lead now of Lewis, now of Clark, though neither captain was ever far from the scene, and never out of mind.

A Distinct Relationship With Each Person in the Trinity

How does a believer relate to the living God who has revealed himself in three persons—Father, Son, and Holy Spirit?

The name of God is the focus of an encounter with Him. His name reveals something of His nature and character, and also His relationship with us. When God spoke to Moses out of a burning bush, telling Moses that He was sending him to Pharaoh to bring the enslaved Israelites out of Egypt, He told Moses the name by which the Israelites would know Him throughout the period of the Old Testament, *Yahweh* (Exodus 3:10–15, Jerusalem Bible). The Israelites considered the name so holy that they would not even speak it aloud. When they read from their scrolls, they would say *Adonai* ("Lord") instead. Most English Bibles translate *Yahweh* as LORD.

In the Old Testament, God is described as father-like, but in the New Testament His primary name becomes Father. Jesus taught His disciples to address the great and holy Yahweh as *Father*. The fruit of Christ's redemption is that the wall of separation between God and man is removed, and "we have peace with God through our Lord Jesus Christ" (Romans 5:1). This is not just a fact to be accepted as true; it is a reality to be experienced. There will be times in our life journey when we will be particularly occupied with the heavenly *Father* in a personal way. We will address our prayers to Him, giving first place to His name, His kingdom, and His will, as Jesus taught His disciples: "Our Father in heaven, hallowed be Your name. Your kingdom come. Your will be done On earth as it is in heaven" (Luke 11:2 NKJV). Through some experience, we may become aware of our need for the Father's love, or aware of His plan and provision for us, and speak our thanks to Him. Or, we may trace the pattern of His purpose in the words of Scripture. The Bible is the priceless gift of the Father, His authoritative "Letter of Instruction" for our life journey. In these and other ways, we may experience the reality of God in His distinctive identity as *Father*.

Rich as it is, the name *Father* does not exhaust all that God has chosen to reveal to us about himself. In Jesus Christ comes further revelation, of which the Father says, "This is my Son, whom I love; with him I am well pleased. Listen to him!" (Matthew 17:5). In His distinctive identity as *Son*, the God who is forever One reveals the mystery that within the Godhead there are distinct persons, separate but not separated.

There will be times when we Ride the River that the Son, Jesus Christ, will particularly command our attention. The persons of the Holy Trinity are coequal in divinity and majesty; this truth is firmly rooted in the New Testament. Jesus said, "I and the Father are one" (John 10:30); the name of each of the divine persons was to be spoken without distinction at the baptism of new believers, "in the name of the Father and of the Son and of the Holy Spirit" (Matthew 28:19). Yet it is also true that the New Testament focuses predominantly on Jesus Christ. This is natural because the New Testament is essentially the account of the salvation that was accomplished through His life, death, and resurrection.

It seems natural for believers in New Testament times (and this carries over for believers today) to give somewhat more attention to their relationship with the Son, Jesus Christ. It is because of Him that we come into relationship with the triune God. The relationship with Jesus does not exclude a distinct relationship with the Father or with the Holy Spirit, but it will predominate for the most part. We are particularly close to the Son; we are members of His body; we are the bride of Christ (Ephesians 5:30–32).

There will be times in our life journey, for example, when we head into a dangerous stretch of rapids with quiet confidence that the Lord Jesus is in command. Or, in a time of discouragement, we sense His sheltering embrace. Or, we experience His gentle but firm authority when, as *Mediator*, He deals concretely with sins and failures that the Holy Spirit has brought to light: "You have come . . . to Jesus the mediator of a new covenant, and to the sprinkled blood that speaks a better word than the blood of Abel. See to it that you do not refuse Him who speaks" (Hebrews 12:23–25). As the Captain of our salvation, Jesus Christ deals with sin in the only way that sin can be dealt with effectively, through repentance and forgiveness. He makes no provision for us to drag along heavy loads of sin and guilt on our life journey: "I write this to you so that you will not sin. But if anybody does sin, we have one who speaks to the Father in our defense—Jesus Christ, the Righteous One. He is the atoning sacrifice for our sins" (1 John 2:1–2). From first to last, He is our loving Bridegroom, intent on leading His bride to become "a radiant church, without stain or wrinkle or any other blemish, but holy and blameless" (Ephesians 5:27).

And there will be times, as we Ride the River, when we experience the leadership of the living God in His distinctive identity as *the Holy Spirit*.

The Holy Spirit may come alongside to equip us or guide us in the face of a new, unexpected, or difficult situation. Or, He may counsel us to maintain silence, to wait on Him and His working. His style of command is not stereotyped. It is strategic and specific to the situation. He may call for a manifestation of divine power, such as a healing or miracle. "The father [of Publius] was sick in bed, suffering from fever and dysentery. Paul went in to see him and, after prayer, placed his hands on him and healed him" (Acts 28:8). In other situations, He may inspire us to press on, enduring more pain than we ever imagined possible, mindful that no other options are possible at this stage of the expedition. Lewis and Clark often expressed admiration for the way that the Corps of Discovery endured hardship. In late June of 1805, Lewis wrote, "The fatigue of these poor fellows is incredible. They are limping from the soreness of their feet. Yet no one complains. All go on with cheerfulness." To be keenly aware of the leadership of the Holy Spirit instills a sense of purpose and destiny that encourages us to slog through difficult circumstances. This awareness releases a joy and cheerfulness that makes no human sense, but the Spirit assures us that we are proceeding on toward the Father's goal.

The Holy Spirit's leadership involves something of a paradox. On the one hand, He produces concrete results in our lives. If, for example, "Husbands, love your wives, just as Christ loved the church" (Ephesians 5:25) touches a man's heart and conscience, he cannot simply decide to "do it" on his own. He must turn his desire to be a better husband over to the Holy Spirit, trusting the Spirit to make him the kind of husband that God wants him to be. A man can change some of his outward behavior, and this may be helpful, but only the Holy Spirit can bring about deep changes that produce Christlike character. The whole business of *sanctification*—conforming our life to the pattern of Christ's life—is a work of the Holy Spirit. In a deep and personal way, He works into our life the will of the Father and the redemptive work of the Son. The same holds true for our *prayers*. By themselves, our prayers are simply words. Under the leadership of the Holy Spirit, they become *power*. The Holy Spirit has sometimes been called "the Executor of the Trinity." He makes things happen. His leadership raises our expectation that God will be powerfully present and active in our everyday life.

On the other hand, the *way* that the Holy Spirit exercises leadership can sometimes be puzzling and frustrating. Much of the time He operates at a very deep level within us, deeper than our thoughts, or feelings, or will. Also, He leads according to His own clock and calendar. And His leadership takes into account the plan and purpose of the heavenly Father in a fuller way than we realize or even know about.

Responding to the leadership of the Holy Spirit requires many *acts of faith* on our part. We must continually release our hopes and prayers and longings to Him, trusting that His excellent leadership is at work within us. As a leader, the Holy Spirit's supernatural presence evokes great expectations, yet His sovereign ways often require us to wait. Klaus Hess, a spiritual father to several renewal groups in Germany following World War II, described these as times of "holy waiting."

Does It Make a Difference?

What difference does it make to have a distinct awareness of each of the persons of the Holy Trinity during our life journey? The practical outcome is twofold.

The first outcome is the more familiar: we receive a fuller revelation of God—of what He is like and what He is up to. In revealing His triune identity, God has given us *knowledge* of himself that is richer and fuller than was known before.

As early as the sixth century the church expressed a sophisticated doctrine of the Holy Trinity. The coequality of Father, Son, and Holy Spirit was established doctrine, as expressed in the Athanasian Creed:

> This is the true Christian faith, that we worship one God in three persons and three persons in one God without confusing the persons or dividing the divine substance.
>
> For the Father is one person, the Son is another, and the Holy Spirit is still another, but there is one Godhead of the Father and of the Son and of the Holy Spirit, equal in glory and coequal in majesty.[13]

The three persons of the Trinity have been anchored in the formal teaching of the church through the centuries. The Nicene Creed ascribes worship to all three of the divine persons, ". . . the Holy Spirit, who with the Father and the Son together is worshiped and glorified." Theologians have written volumes on the person of Jesus Christ, fewer on the person of the Father, fewer still on the person of the Holy Spirit. Yet they have firmly held to the doctrine of the Trinity and discoursed on it with learning. Teaching on the Trinity has defined the boundary between biblical faith and a host of heresies.

Fortunately, the three persons of the Trinity have also been a distinct focus in the worship life of the church. From earliest times, Christians have opened and closed their services of worship "In the Name of the Father, and of the Son, and of the Holy Spirit." The medieval saint Mechthild of Magdeburg (1212–1280) taught the life of prayer to the novices of her order. On her deathbed she prayed, "Father, I thank Thee that Thou hast made me; Jesus Christ, I thank Thee that Thou hast redeemed me; Holy Spirit, I thank Thee that Thou hast sanctified me. Holy Trinity, grant me a merciful death, release me from every burden."[14]

Believers have recited faith in each of the persons of the Trinity in liturgy and hymns through the centuries.

> Father most holy, merciful and tender;
> Jesus our Savior, with the Father reigning;
> Spirit all kindly, Advocate, Defender,
> Light never waning. (Latin hymn, 10th century)

> Heavenly Father we appreciate You . . .
> Son of God we magnify You . . .
> Holy Spirit what a comfort You are . . .
>   (Praise chorus, contemporary)

But how much of this finds its way into our everyday lives? A distinct awareness of the three persons of the Trinity has a second outcome: a fuller *experience* of God in everyday life.

Do we wake each morning with the awareness that our life is under the active, coequal leadership of our divine Captains, according to the will of the Father? *This is the reality on which the practical outcome of our life as Christians depends.*

In the divine economy, a full experience of the triune God

depends on encountering each of the persons of the Trinity, for the divine persons advocate not themselves but One another.

Jesus said, "I am the way and the truth and the life. *No one comes to the Father except through me*" (John 14:6). The Father remains distant apart from an encounter with Jesus.

Likewise, apart from a revelation by the Father, Jesus' true identity is shrouded in uncertainty. For a pious Jew, trained from childhood to confess, "Hear, O Israel: The Lord our God, the Lord is *one*" (Deuteronomy 6:4), it took something on the order of an earthquake to entertain the idea that God could in some way be more, or other, than One. The "earthquake" was a revelation from God the Father. When Peter said to Jesus, "You are the Christ, the Son of the living God," Jesus responded, "This was not revealed to you by man, but by my Father in heaven" (Matthew 16:16–17).

The revelation of Jesus depends further upon an encounter with the Holy Spirit. Jesus said, "When he, the Spirit of truth, comes . . . he will bring glory to me by taking from what is mine and making it known to you" (John 16:13–14). Apart from the work of the Holy Spirit, a "relationship with Jesus Christ" may be a mental concept, but it will not be real; the realistic and deeply personal relationship with Jesus Christ that the Bible describes can only be worked in us by the Holy Spirit.

Our experience of the Holy Spirit, in turn, depends upon an encounter with Jesus; the Bible says that "[Jesus] will baptize you with the Holy Spirit" (Mark 1:8).

To know and experience the different persons of the Trinity has a practical outcome. As we Ride the River of God's plan for our lives, divine leadership will be exercised now by one person of the Trinity, then by Another, according to divine strategy. This is not essentially a matter of our choosing, but of discerning God's purpose in the present situation. It is like children in a family following the lead now of the mother, now of the father, according to the business at hand.

The alternating leadership of the persons of the Holy Trinity helps keep our experience of God from getting in a spiritual rut. For example, because He sees that we need to experience His love in a special way, God the Father may draw close to us for a time. But the flesh is quick to seize on spiritual experience and reduce it to a formula that we can manipulate at will. According to His own wisdom and timing, the Father will shift the focus of leadership to another of the divine persons; a quiet time with the Father may give place to a time of intense preparation for ministry under the leadership of the Holy Spirit.

In the latter half of the twentieth century a spiritual movement that came to be known as "charismatic renewal" swept around the world and into every Christian denomination. What was happening? Essentially this: God was speaking to millions of believers who knew something of the presence and leadership of Jesus Christ, and saying, *You need to become more attentive to the leadership of the Holy Spirit. Jesus himself is the one who baptizes with the Holy Spirit. Listen to Him.*

God the Father, Jesus Christ the Son, and the Holy Spirit each play a distinctive role, equipping and leading believers in their life journey. God did not leave the direction and success of the venture up to the good will, good intentions, knowledge and learning, moral resolve, or determined effort of man. Nor did He put the expedition under the leadership of just one person of the Trinity. The expedition is grounded in the full participation and the unshakable unity of the Holy Trinity.

The Father's personal plan for your life, and the active leadership of Jesus Christ and the Holy Spirit, gives stability and certainty to your life journey. Not the certainty of something predictable, but the certainty of confidence in the Ones who lead you. This confidence is joined to an alert flexibility. The ways of our divine Captains are strategic, sometimes full of surprise, because they are always pushing forward into the unmapped territory of your life. Come what may, they proceed on toward the goal appointed by the Father.

A United Partnership

The night before His crucifixion, Jesus spoke at length to His disciples, preparing them for what would happen when He returned to heaven. "It is for your good that I am going away. Unless I go away, the Counselor will not come to you; but if I go, I will send him to you" (John 16:7). He wanted His disciples to recognize, receive, and honor the Holy Spirit when He came. Clearly, the Holy Spirit was a person distinct from Jesus—*another* Counselor (John 14:16)—yet fully united with Him.

No one can read Jesus' "Farewell Discourse" to His disciples (John 14–17) and miss the sense of *high regard* that Jesus expresses for the Holy Spirit. He would never countenance any disregard, or downgrading, of the Holy Spirit by any disciples of His.

In a little more than seven weeks, these disciples would receive the Holy Spirit and they would launch out on the adventure of their lives. They would experience the leadership of Jesus Christ and the Holy Spirit in ways both remarkable and ordinary. They would receive and care for one another like members of a family. They would turn the world upside down (Acts 17:6 NKJV).

CHAPTER FOUR
THE CANDIDATES

*When you Ride the River, a relationship with God the Father, with
Jesus Christ, and with the Holy Spirit can be clearly established,
maintained, and deepened. What is missing or deficient
can be made up.*

LEWIS AND CLARK had no lack of candidates for the Voyage of
Discovery. According to Stephen Ambrose, a sense of sheer exci-
temnt spread through the country west of the Allegheny Mountains when news of the expedition became known: "What young
frontiersman could resist such an opportunity? It was the ultimate
adventure."[1]

Before the two captains met in the Indiana Territory, each of
them began to interview candidates for the expedition, subject to
the approval of the other. At one point Clark wrote Lewis that
several "gentlemen's sons" had applied to him. He declined to accept them; they were not prepared for the discipline that the journey would require. Lewis wrote back, "I am well pleased that you
have not admitted or encouraged the young gentlemen you mention. We must set our faces against all such applications." This was
no expedition for dabblers thinking to add a touch of adventure
to their lives.

The men chosen for the Voyage of Discovery came with a
variety of talents and skills, but they had one thing in common:
they were ready to follow Lewis and Clark into an unexplored wilderness.

The call to become a Christian has never changed. It is the

same today as it was when Jesus walked the roads of Galilee. To any who would become disciples, He says, "Follow me."

How the Early Church Took On New Candidates

The Bible recounts how people became Christians in the early church. They were drawn into a life of discipleship by a chain of five links:

repenting toward God
believing in the Lord Jesus
being baptized in water
receiving the Holy Spirit
becoming part of the fellowship of believers

The links were closely related, yet each was distinct. Together they formed a whole, the first steps in a life committed to the plan and purpose of God. They could occur close together, or over a period of time; they could also occur in differing sequence. David Pawson, who has a ministry to church leaders in the United Kingdom and is the author of two books I refer to in some detail, makes the point that the important thing was "their completion rather than their coincidence."[2]

Notice first that each of the links was distinctly *relational*. The links were not designed to help a person do a better job of living the same old independent life. Their purpose was to establish and strengthen the *new* life, that is, the life maintained and directed by the indwelling presence of the triune God. These initiatory events ushered people into a life union with the Holy Trinity and with other believers that would launch them on a life journey planned by God and led by Jesus Christ and the Holy Spirit.

The new life in Christ was not meant to be a scrubbed-up version of the old individualistic life. Here we encounter a fundamental insight—and a fatal flaw—in the way the Christian life is sometimes taught. The presentation of how a person comes to salvation is clear and effective, but how a person is empowered to live the Christian life day by day is misconstrued.

This flawed presentation begins with the right question: "How does a person come into a right relationship with God?" (How is a person "justified"?) It serves up the right answer: "We have put our faith in Christ Jesus that we may be justified by faith in Christ and not by observing the law, because by observing the law no one will be justified" (Galatians 2:16). This of course is sound biblical teaching: "salvation by grace, not by works." So far, so good.

But then comes the question, "What do I do now?" And the fatal flaw follows: "I must live a good Christian life"—with the accent on I.

The Danish philosopher Søren Kierkegaard characterized the Christian life as "a striving born of gratitude."[3] This may describe how a person feels under the press of a difficult duty, and it may express in some measure the love one feels toward God. Such striving, however, does not point to the objective power center of the Christian life.

If the motivation for Christian living is simply a striving born of gratitude, you have "works righteousness" on the installment plan—saved now, pay later. You believe in Jesus and receive the gift of salvation right now—and along with it your Gratitude Payment Book. For every good work you get a gratitude stamp to paste in your payment book. You are saved the moment you believe in Christ, but you pay for it the rest of your life with acts of gratitude. According to this misconception, salvation is a matter of what God does, but *living* the Christian life is very much a matter of what *you* do.[4]

The apostle Paul did not see gratitude, even for the gift of salvation, as the motivating power of the Christian life. He opened and closed his great letter to the Romans calling for the "obedience that comes from *faith*" (Romans 1:5, 16:26). For Paul, this meant nothing less than obedience that flows out of a living union with Christ. "I have been crucified with Christ and I no longer live, but Christ lives in me. The life I live in the body, I live by faith in the Son of God, who loved me and gave himself for me" (Galatians 2:20). It is not human gratitude but the living presence of Jesus Christ and the Holy Spirit—their leadership in our everyday life—that is the power center of the Christian life.

To live the Christian life, it is not enough to remember how much we have to be grateful for. We must lay hold upon the union of our life with the life of the triune God, and thus live out of that mysterious reality. Only then can we grasp the true meaning of the many commands, admonitions, and imperatives in the New Testament. These commands are not addressed to ordinary people in the world. They are addressed to "new creatures in Christ," people whose lives have been united to the life of the triune God. In a sense, New Testament admonitions are addressed not simply to the believer but to the indwelling Spirit with whom the believer's life has been united. To *such* people, the Bible can say things like, "Live a life of love, just as Christ loved us and gave himself up for us. . . . Among you there must not be even a hint of sexual immorality, or of any kind of impurity, or of greed, because these are improper for God's holy people" (Ephesians 5:2–3). Addressing words like these to people who do not know God's indwelling presence would be as pointless as telling a man with no legs to line up for a marathon. The New Testament ethic is not a simple human possibility. *It describes the life of people who are in living union with the living God.* In the New Testament, the new life is not a catalog of improvements on the old life. It is the death knell of the old life. What follows is a new creation.

The change is so radical that it would not overstate the case to describe believers as a new species on the earth. The newness consists in this, that the life of the believer is joined to the indwelling life of the triune God. One can speak of the old life as *my* life. When the new comes, one can only say, with Paul, "It is no longer I who live, but Christ lives in me" (Galatians 2:20 NKJV).

In the New Testament, each of the links that draws a person into a life of discipleship is designed to establish and strengthen one's relationship with a person of the Holy Trinity, or with the company of believers.

Repenting toward God breaks down the wall of separation between the individual and God, the Father makes His home with the believer, and the peace of God displaces enmity and strife.

Believing in the Lord Jesus brings the believer into union with the Savior and Deliverer appointed by the Father.

Baptism unites the believer with the death and resurrection of the Lord Jesus and with the fellowship of believers.

Receiving the Holy Spirit brings the presence of the third person of the Trinity into the innermost life of the believer.

Becoming part of the fellowship of believers unites the believer with other members of God's Corps of Discovery—those committed to follow the plan of God under the leadership of Jesus Christ and the Holy Spirit.

A keen sense of purpose and direction characterized the early church. It rested on the living, day-by-day relationship that members had with the Father in heaven, with the Lord Jesus Christ, with the Holy Spirit, and with one another.

Our first concern is to look closely at the pattern and teaching that we find in the Bible. For the moment, we postpone the question of how to apply it in practical situations today.

The primary source for seeing how people became followers of Jesus is the book of Acts, written by Luke, who also wrote the Gospel of Luke. In describing various incidents in which people came into the faith, Luke often uses *synecdoche*, a figure of speech in which a part of something stands for the whole. He mentions one or more of the five links that particularly describe the situation he wants to present. These links stand for the whole chain; the other links are implied or taken for granted.

For example, when the apostle Peter spoke to a group of Gentiles in the household of a Roman centurion, Cornelius, the Bible mentions two of the links:

While Peter was saying this, the Holy Spirit fell on all who heard the word. And the believers from among the circum-cised who came with Peter were amazed, because the gift of the Holy Spirit had been poured out even on the Gentiles. For they heard them speaking in tongues and extolling God. Then Peter declared, "Can any one forbid water for baptizing these people who have *received the Holy Spirit* just as we have?" And he commanded them to *be baptized* in the name of Jesus Christ. (Acts 10:44–48 RSV)

In the next chapter of Acts, Peter reports this event to the other apostles, back in Jerusalem. Now the Bible characterizes the happening by referring to two other links not mentioned in the previous chapter:

If then God gave the same gift to them as he gave to us when we *believed in the Lord Jesus Christ*, who was I that I could withstand God? When they heard this they were si-lenced. And they glorified God, saying, "Then to the Gentiles also God has granted *repentance* unto life." (Acts 11:17–18 RSV)

In the two reports of this event, Acts specifically mentions four links. The fifth, becoming part of the fellowship of believers, would be implied. In other cases, fewer links may be mentioned—sometimes only one—and the others taken for granted. This style is consistent throughout the book of Acts.

Candidates EXPERIENCED Each Link

The early Christians expected new believers to experience each of the links in a noticeable way.

The first link, repenting toward God, brought a person out of hiding, as it were (see Genesis 3:8), into a life-changing encounter with his Creator. It brought about observable *change*—change in one's thinking, in one's attitudes, in one's life. John the Baptist, whose baptism was a precursor of Jesus' baptism, thundered the challenge, "Bear fruit that befits repentance" (Matthew 3:8 RSV). Mere words or feelings would not satisfy. When Saul of Tarsus (later called Paul) became a believer, the report spread like a prairie fire through the Christian community: "The man who formerly persecuted us is now preaching the faith he once tried to destroy" (Galatians 1:23). His repentance and conversion dramatically changed his behavior.

The second link, believing in the Lord Jesus, meant a radical new life-focus on Jesus Christ, a belief in the apostles' testimony about His life, death, and resurrection. When a frightened jailer in Philippi asked the apostle Paul what he must do to be saved, Paul answered in the simplest terms possible: "Believe in the Lord Jesus, and you will be saved" (Acts 16:31). And, ultimately, it meant obedience to Jesus as one's Savior and Lord. When Paul told two Roman officials, Agrippa and Festus, about his encounter with Christ, which led to his becoming a Christian, he particularly mentioned the issue of obedience: "I was not disobedient to the vision from heaven" (Acts 26:19).

The third link, baptism, signaled a visible identification of the new believer with Jesus Christ. The candidate publicly acknowledged Him as Lord, and as Savior from the bondage of sin. In his sermon on the Day of Pentecost, Peter specifically linked baptism with the forgiveness of sins (Acts 2:38).

More prominently and publicly than any of the other links, baptism grafted a person into the Christian community, the body of Christ. "We were all baptized by one Spirit into one body" (1 Corinthians 12:13). The one objective sign uniting all Christians is the name of Christ, which has been placed upon them in baptism.[5]

Within the Christian community, baptism was understood as a divine action, a means by which a new believer was united with Jesus Christ in His death and resurrection. "Don't you know that all of us who were baptized into Christ Jesus were baptized into his death? We were therefore buried with him through baptism into death in order that, just as Christ was raised from the dead through the glory of the Father, we too may live a new life" (Romans 6:3–4).

The fourth link, receiving the Holy Spirit, involved a conscious, identifiable encounter with the third person of the Trinity. John the Baptist prophesied that Jesus would "baptize [His followers] in the Holy Spirit" (Matthew 3:11; Mark 1:8; Luke 3:16; John 1:33). Jesus spoke the same prophecy to His disciples after His resurrection, on the day He ascended to heaven (Acts 1:5). Both of these prophecies compared and contrasted Jesus baptizing people in the Holy Spirit and John baptizing people in the Jordan River. The event was objective, identifiable.

The apostle Paul once met some disciples in Ephesus. His straightforward question to them anticipated a simple yes-or-no answer: "Did you receive the Holy Spirit when you believed?" (Acts 19:2). When people received the Holy Spirit in the New Testament, they knew it; they could tell other people about it.

Other people could also verify the event. When the disciples received the Holy Spirit on the Day of Pentecost, a curious crowd gathered. Peter spoke to them, "God has raised this Jesus to life. . . . He has received from the Father the promised Holy Spirit and has poured out what you now *see* and *hear*" (Acts 2:32–33). The event was not purely private. People looking on could see and hear that something had happened.

The pattern is consistent throughout the New Testament—receiving the Holy Spirit was an objective experience. "While Peter was still speaking . . . the Holy Spirit came on all who heard the message. The circumcised believers who had come with Peter were astonished that the gift of the Holy Spirit had been poured out even on the Gentiles. For they *heard* them speaking in tongues and praising God" (Acts 10:44–45).[6]

The fifth link, becoming part of the fellowship, followed as a natural consequence of baptism. Individual believers needed the fellowship of other believers for their own development, refinement, encouragement, and protection. When Peter spoke about Jesus to a large crowd in Jerusalem on the Day of Pentecost, "those who accepted his message were baptized, and about three thousand were added to their number that day. They devoted themselves to the apostles' teaching and to the fellowship, to the break-ing of bread and to prayer" (Acts 2:41–42; see also 8:12 and 9:18).

The book of Acts does not present these five links as "require-ments for salvation" in a narrow sense. Where salvation is in view, the gospel comes across with the greatest simplicity: "Everyone who calls on the name of the Lord will be saved" (Acts 2:21); "Believe in the Lord Jesus, and you will be saved" (Acts 16:31).

The book of Acts as a whole, however, focuses not simply on salvation but on carrying out the commission of Jesus: "You shall be my witnesses in Jerusalem and in all Judea and Samaria and to the end of the earth" (Acts 1:8 RSV). The five links show us how God prepares and empowers people to follow the river of His will, under the leadership of Jesus Christ and the Holy Spirit.

None of the Links Was Left Out

It was important to the early Christian fellowship that none of the links was left out of a new believer's experience. The book of Acts shows clearly that the five links, though related, are neverthe-less distinct from one another. None of them happened automat-ically or unconsciously. In some cases, one or another link was lacking in a person's experience. When that was the case, the apos-tles took steps to correct the situation, to fill in or make up what was missing.

For example, when Philip, one of the deacons in the early church, preached in Samaria, a revival broke out. Many people believed and were baptized. However, they did not receive the Holy Spirit. Two of the apostles, Peter and John, came from Jeru-salem and "prayed for them that they might receive the Holy Spirit. For as yet He had fallen upon none of them. They had only been baptized in the name of the Lord Jesus. Then they laid hands on them, and they received the Holy Spirit" (Acts 8:15–16 NKJV).

The record mentions two links: people believed and were bap-tized. It recounts how a third link, receiving the Holy Spirit, was lacking; the apostles took steps to make up for it.

In the case of one convert, the link of repentance was also weak or missing. Simon, who had practiced sorcery in Samaria, believed and was baptized. "When Simon saw that the Spirit was given at the laying on of the apostles' hands, he offered them money and said, 'Give me also this ability so that everyone on whom I lay my hands may receive the Holy Spirit' " (Acts 8:18–19). Peter, however, rebuked him and told him to repent; he discerned that Simon was still in the clutches of sin.

In Ephesus, as we have seen, the apostle Paul met a group of "disciples" (another word for "believers" or "Christians," in Acts). He discovered that they had received the baptism and teaching of John the Baptist. Paul told them, "John's baptism was a baptism of repentance. He told the people to believe in the one coming after him, that is, in Jesus. On hearing this, they were baptized into the name of the Lord Jesus. When Paul placed his hands on them, the Holy Spirit came on them, and they spoke in tongues and prophesied" (Acts 19:4–6). These people had taken some steps along the pathway of discipleship, but their faith, their baptism, and their experience of the Holy Spirit were inadequate or lacking. Paul took steps to make up what was missing.

The practice of the apostles was simple and consistent: they saw to it that candidates for the Christian faith were joined to the Lord by a strong chain of experienced truth, a chain of five links, not one of which should be missing.

Recovering the Practice of the Apostles

From the days of the apostles, these five links continued to be a part of Christian faith and teaching. Catholic Benedictine scholar Kilian McDonnell has traced this pattern of Christian initiation through the first eight centuries of the Christian era.[7] Two developments, however, watered down the practice of the early church.

First, the five links have been given differing degrees of emphasis at different times or in different parts of the church. The early church established no rank or standing among the five links.

The process was seen as a whole. Each link was distinct, each was necessary; together they comprised a unity.

Today, each of the links has champions, in various churches, movements, or Christian traditions. Repentance, often including public confession, characterizes certain renewal movements, such as the East Africa revival. Baptism receives strong emphasis in churches with a sacramental tradition. Believing in Jesus holds first place in evangelical circles. Most groups stress the importance of Christian fellowship, though in differing ways. Pentecostal and charismatic churches underscore the need to receive the Holy Spirit.

These emphases on one link or another do not necessarily exclude the other links; rather, the tendency is that they assume them, take them for granted—something the early church never did. The early church understood that becoming a disciple was a process consisting of several distinct parts. It did not elevate one part of the process over the others; all were needed. It maintained a balance often absent in the church today.

The second thing that has happened is that intellectual concepts have displaced the *experience* of being drawn into a life of discipleship. People are taught a theological belief system. To have "faith" has come to mean that you agree with certain doctrines. Instruction is a vital part of initiation, but its purpose is not simply to add to our store of knowledge. It is meant to help us *know* and *live under* the leadership of our divine Captains when we Ride the River. The essence of divine guidance is the day-by-day business of following our living Lord.

Make Up What Is Missing!

Lewis and Clark saw to it that deficiencies in the men's basic skills were made up. For example, once the Corps of Discovery left St. Louis, the rifle would become the basic tool of survival—for obtaining food and defending against possible enemies. While they camped north of St. Louis in the winter of 1803–04, the captains assigned the men to target practice under the watchful eye of Sergeant John Ordway. Ordway expected them, on sudden command, to hit a target at a distance of fifty yards. Being a crack shot with a rifle was no optional extra in the Corps of Discovery. It was necessary for survival.

Early in the journey, one of the privates, George Shannon, was sent to hunt for some horses that had wandered off. He got lost. By the time he found his way back to the main party, sixteen days later, Shannon had nearly starved to death. Clark wrote that "he was not yet a first rate hunter." Some months later this kind of deficiency had been largely made up in the Corps of Discovery. Lewis noted in his journal, "Most of the party have become very expert with the rifle."

The church today needs to revive the ministry of the apostles, to "make up what is missing." This is nothing new. Pastors and spiritual counselors often try to help believers make up deficiencies in their spiritual experience; these efforts need to become more focused, more intentional. This means recovering both the *balance* and the *experience* of the early church.

Balance means that no link in the scriptural pattern will be ignored, certainly not denied; no link will be unduly elevated, nor will any link be downgraded.

Experience means what the word normally means, "something personally encountered, undergone, or lived through." This is the very opposite of the popular misconception that "religious experience" is simply a matter of private inner feelings. Of course, any experience involves our own inner awareness of it, but we normally focus attention on the objective "something" we encounter, not our inner awareness of it. When the apostles tell about their "experience" of God, they are not simply describing their inner feelings; they are reporting an objective encounter with the living God. Reviving the apostolic ministry of "making up what is missing" means recovering the kind of experience of God the Father, of Jesus Christ, and of the Holy Spirit that happened in the early church.

◐ Baptism

The easiest place to illustrate "making up what is missing" may be with regard to baptism. It is the link that is most clearly evident to an observer.

William Booth, founder of the Salvation Army, took the Christian gospel to the outcasts of society. *The History of Christianity* makes the observation, "The Army was perhaps the only Christian movement to reach the wavelength of the masses in the nineteenth century."[8] Booth, however, did not baptize his converts.

One of my favorite poems is "General William Booth Enters Into Heaven," by Vachel Lindsay.[9] The poet vividly portrays the heavenly scene—

Booth led boldly with his big bass drum
Saints smiled gravely and they said, "He's come!"

Lindsay goes on to describe the scene; rank on rank they come, following Booth into heaven—lepers, drug fiends, prostitutes—the dregs of society that Booth and the Salvation Army won to the Christian faith. He concludes:

In an instant all that blear review
Marched on spotless, clad in raiment new.
The lame were straightened, withered limbs uncurled
And blind eyes opened on a new sweet world.

What about William Booth and the Salvation Army? Allowing for poetic license, did Vachel Lindsay get it right—did they "march on spotless, clad in raiment new"? Were they "real Christians"? Were they "saved"?

It seems shameless even to pose such questions when one considers of the ministry of William Booth and the Salvation Army, which continues to this day.

What would you do if you met a Salvation Army convert and found out that she was not baptized, since the Salvation Army does not practice water baptism? Would non-baptism nullify her standing as a Christian?

I once encountered this situation. The person was not a member of the Salvation Army, but of my own Lutheran church. I stopped in at a meeting of one of the women's groups in the congregation. They were studying the topic of baptism. A bit hesitantly, one of the members spoke up and said, "Pastor, I've never been baptized."

She was a longtime, faithful member of the church. When she had become a member, the pastor may simply have assumed that she was baptized. Her natural shyness may have prevented her from pursuing the matter. In any case, I said, "We can do it right now." So, with the other members of the group standing witness, Helen was baptized. Some years later we were talking about it. Helen said, "I had always felt that something was missing."

It was not a complicated matter. Any other pastor would have handled the situation in much the same way. *We made up what was missing.*

Was Helen a Christian before she was baptized? Would she have gone to heaven if she had died three days earlier? Of course! But I would agree with David Pawson that the apostles would never have dreamed of asking such questions. The questions betray a minimum admission mentality: "What is the least I must have in order to get into heaven?" These kinds of questions explain a great deal of the contrast between the ancient and the modern church. The apostles were more concerned about what happens if a person *lives* without baptism than if he *dies* without it.[10]

Three months after the Lewis and Clark expedition got under way, one of its members, Sergeant Charles Floyd, died, apparently from a perforated appendix. He was buried with full military honors. Lewis read the funeral service at graveside. Clark wrote a glowing tribute to him in his journal. There was no doubt that he was a member of the Corps of Discovery, though he shared but little of the journey.

The earliest name given to the Christian community was simply followers of "the Way" (Acts 9:2; 19:9, 23). It was the picture of a journey, not unlike our figure of a voyage of discovery. David

Pawson writes, "I believe that anyone who is already on the Way of salvation and traveling in the right direction is safe with the Lord if they die."[11]

The chain of experience that draws a person into Christian discipleship certainly prepares a person for death, from the very first step. Its primary focus, however, is on life—on the voyage of discovery that lies ahead. Each link in the chain is important for the expedition, or God would not have included it. If one is missing, it can be made up.

Repentance

The objective reality of *change* stands at the center of biblical repentance. Repentance changes one's relationship with God the Father. The breach between man and God is overcome. "We have peace with God through our Lord Jesus Christ" (Romans 5:1).

Repentance goes beyond the popular meaning of the term today—"being sorry" about something. A schoolboy described repentance succinctly, "It's being sorry enough to stop!"[12] Repent means "change the inner man to meet God's will" (Revelation 2:5, AMP). The emotion that one may experience is secondary to the fundamental meaning, which is "a change of mind."

During the winter camp of 1804–05 among the Mandan Indians, the French trader Charbonneau served as an interpreter. Toward spring he said that he would join the Corps of Discovery on its westward trek only on his own conditions: he would not do any of the work, nor stand guard; if miffed by any man, he could leave the expedition and return; he could take along as much provision as he wished to carry.

The captains let him know that setting his own conditions was unacceptable. Three days later Charbonneau had "a change of mind." He begged Clark to "excuse his simplicity" and take him into service. He would accompany the Corps of Discovery on the captains' terms, do everything they wished him to do. On this basis, the captains took him on.

The call to repentance deals with sin and the need for forgiveness, but not as an isolated reality. It points beyond itself. It is a step, a necessary step, in preparing candidates to participate in the voyage of discovery. It is a "change of mind" that asks God to "excuse our simplicity" and take us into service on His terms, not ours.

Two Captains command the voyage of discovery. All the rest of us are non-coms or privates. Repentance reminds us who is in charge. Repentance gives up independence, rebellion, and self-will, and redirects our lives to follow where our divine Captains lead us.

On the Day of Pentecost, the apostle Peter spoke to a crowd of several thousand people, telling them to "change their mind" in regard to Jesus of Nazareth. Seven weeks earlier, some in that crowd had seen Jesus executed on a Roman cross. Now Peter tells them, "God has raised this Jesus to life . . . and made [Him] both Lord and Christ" (Acts 2:32, 36). Whatever opinion they may have had about Jesus, they must now recognize that God has conferred great authority on Him.

The call went out to everyone. Some in the crowd may have liked or admired Jesus. Some may have been too busy with their own affairs to take much notice of Him. Some may have followed Him for a time to hear Him teach and see Him heal the sick. Some may have clamored with the mob, "Crucify him! Crucify him!" Still others may have shrugged Him off as a misguided prophet. No matter—now *everyone* was told to accept the will and decree of God the Father, recognizing Jesus as Lord and Christ.

What do you do when God designates someone as Lord and Christ—someone whom you may have dismissed in one way or another?

The sense of wrongdoing, of having missed the mark, of having offended God must have hung like a dark cloud that Pentecost Day. "The people . . . were cut to the heart and said to Peter and the other apostles, 'Brothers, what shall we do?' " Peter put his finger on what they needed: "Repent and be baptized, every one of you, in the name of Jesus Christ for the forgiveness of your sins." Then, in a dramatic shift of focus from the past to the future, he said: "And you will receive the gift of the Holy Spirit. The promise is for you and your children and all who are far off—for all whom the Lord our God will call" (Acts 2:37–39).

Unfortunately, many Christians have been signed on without hearing a word about repentance. They launch upriver toting so much baggage from the past that they are ill-equipped for the hard work and flexible maneuvering required by the Captains. They may have been raised in homes where believing in God was accepted without much reflection or meaningful experience, or in churches that spoke only to affirm and encourage, never to correct or rebuke. Some may have responded to an appeal to "accept Jesus," but the question of sin and the need of forgiveness was scarcely mentioned, and then only in the most general terms.

Where the step of repentance has been brushed over lightly, or skipped altogether, it can be made up. How can this be done?

Private Confession

The "inner healing" movement, which has spread through many churches in recent years, has helped many people. Old emotional wounds, festering in the memory, have been healed through prayer and personal ministry. Originally, however, the movement included an equally strong emphasis on repentance and forgiveness.

The mother of the movement was Agnes Sanford, with her original concept, "the healing of the emotions."[13] In her later years, she said that the inner healing movement had become unbalanced by focusing only on people's hurts and their need for healing, with no attention to people's sins and their need for forgiveness. Her own emphasis had always been two-pronged, which she illustrated with the hymn verse:

There is a balm in Gilead to make the wounded whole.
There is a balm in Gilead to heal the sin-sick soul.

Agnes Sanford said the personal experience that opened this up for her came "in a way that seemed strange indeed to me at first, simply because it was so ordinary—so old—so absolutely fundamental! Through the advice of a friend, I tried the Confessional."[14]

Protestants have tended to dismiss private confession as a "Catholic thing." The practice, however, is rooted in Scripture: "Confess your sins to each other and pray for each other so that you may be healed" (James 5:16).

The *Marburger Kreis*, a Protestant group in Germany with an evangelistic ministry, conducts retreats for business and professional people who often have little or no background in any church. It includes private confession as an integral part of its presentation of the Christian faith. Its longtime leader, Arthur Richter, once said, "Private confession is the 'wall' we lead them up to. When they get there, they either turn around and walk away, or they spring over it . . . to freedom."[15]

The twelve-step program of Alcoholics Anonymous includes Step Five, "We admitted to God, to ourselves, and to another human being the exact nature of our wrongs."

"The devil loves generalizations and abstractions," writes Lutheran pastor Philip Johnson, "the land of shadows where the contour of our sins remains vague, undefined, unnamed."[16] Where confession is general—"Yes, I'm a sinner; everyone's a sinner"— sin tends to remain general and forgiveness impersonal. Private confession of specific sins personalizes both sin and forgiveness.

When I first put this to a practical test in my own life, I was scared. I had prayed about the matter for some time. I had written out a detailed list of sins, according to the advice of a mature Christian. I made an appointment with Gerhard Frost, one of my seminary professors. The thought kept nagging, *What in the world will he think of me when he hears all this?* That, I realized later, was the devil's temptation.

When I came to the appointment, Pastor Frost's opening words were, "Larry, we sit here as two sinners together."

I had not realized how tense I was; I felt my body relax. *What have I been so uptight about*, I thought to myself. *He's been here too.*

I read my confession to him without much comment and with no great emotion. He laid his hands on my head, prayed for me, and pronounced the forgiveness of sin, according to Scripture. Again, I felt no great emotion. In the days that followed, however, joy and freedom were like two companions walking at my side. Repentance and forgiveness had taken on a fresh reality. *Something lacking had been made up.*

In my experience as a pastor, private confession has proved the most effective way to help people experience the reality of re-pentance and forgiveness. Over many years, I have seen this an-cient practice of the church bring peace and comfort to people under my pastoral care. I have observed that it often gives faith a greater staying power over the long haul. The very fact that it is not an *easy* way may be a good recommendation.

No step in the Christian life should be entered upon lightly. Certain conditions need to be present and observed where private confession is practiced, such as absolute confidentiality, and spiri-tual maturity on the part of the one who hears confession.[17]

Some may find themselves in a congregation or Christian fel-lowship where private confession is not practiced or available. Some may simply prefer a less formal approach. David Pawson in his book *The Normal Christian Birth* offers good practical help in a chapter titled, "Helping Disciples to Repent."[18]

However it is accomplished, repentance and forgiveness need to become more than words in the religious vocabulary. When you Ride the River, there needs to be that companionable nod between you and Jesus Christ, acknowledging that all known sin has been dealt with.

Believing in the Lord Jesus

Two little boys walked along together. One said to the other, "There's no Santa Claus."

"There isn't?" the other responded.

"Nope. It's just a fairy tale. Something your folks cook up."

They trudged along in silence for a few moments, then the second boy said, "Maybe we'd better check out this Jesus business too."

Children are not self-absorbed skeptics. They are down-to-earth pragmatists. They want to know whether this Jesus that people talk about is for real.

Quite a few grown-ups, including some theologians, need to check out where they are in regard to Jesus Christ. There are people today, inside the church as well as outside, whose understanding of the Christian faith is fragmentary and distorted. They may have some knowledge of Jesus Christ, but it has not been galvanized into the experience of personal faith; or, if it once was, it has become dormant. A seminary president once told a group of us that the biggest problem he faced was the erosion of faith among his faculty. He said bluntly: "Many of them no longer believe in a living God."[19]

A "Once Upon a Time" Gospel

Where the foundation is not in place, it needs to be made up. "No one can lay any foundation other than the one already laid, which is Jesus Christ" (1 Corinthians 3:11). For our purposes, at this point I would like to give this foundation a special designation, calling it a "Once Upon a Time" Gospel: "Once upon a time . . . the Son of God came down to earth and lived as a man. He was crucified on a Roman cross, shedding His blood as an atonement for sin. God raised Him from the dead and promised life and salvation to all who put their trust in Him. If you believe in Him, God will forgive your sins and you will go to heaven."

Throughout history, and in many parts of the church today, this truth has been faithfully taught, and it has preserved the church. The Once Upon a Time Gospel is true, and it is essential. The heart of every true believer must sing with the truth of the gospel song, "Sins atoned and heaven gained!"[20] Without the Once Upon a Time Gospel, Jesus is not for real. If this truth is missing, it needs to be made up. The Once Upon a Time Gospel marks the beginning of our life journey. It is not, however, a place to settle down, as though one had completed the journey.

The trouble with a Once Upon a Time Gospel is not in what it says, for it is true. Trouble arises when that is *all* that is said, for that is *not* true. It is not true that the only thing the gospel tells us is that, because of Jesus, God forgives our sin and takes us to heaven. Lutheran pastor Delbert Rossin put it crisply, "There's nothing more to salvation than Jesus, but there's more to Jesus than salvation."[21]

A Once Upon a Time Gospel is too much of a good thing. It fills up the agenda with the Bible's teaching on forgiveness. It focuses on the past, but says almost nothing about how Jesus Christ exercises active leadership in our life today.

Believing in Jesus for the forgiveness of sin is fundamental: you cannot sign on without it. But an unexplored wilderness lies ahead. As certainly as you need Jesus Christ for the forgiveness of sins, you need His active presence as you Ride the River today.

One of the strange teachings that has led the church away from a "Today" Gospel is the idea that if we expect anything more from God than the forgiveness of sins and a home in heaven, we compromise the biblical teaching of "salvation by faith." Theologians will caution the laity that they must content themselves to live by "faith," not "experience."[22]

A church official once said to me, "If God will just forgive my sins and take me to heaven when I die, that's all I dare hope for." He went on to tell me the most incredible story of a struggle he had been through, in which the forgiveness of sins and a home in heaven scarcely figured in the conversation. Here was a major episode in his life, a struggle that almost did him in, and he had no sense that his Savior, Jesus Christ, wanted to do anything more than sit on the riverbank, looking on.

How does a Once Upon a Time Gospel portray the Christian faith? First, it focuses its camera on the past. "Once Upon a Time God came into the world. He lived on earth as a man. He suffered and died for all our sins, then He rose from the dead." At this point, the Once Upon a Time Gospel does a fast pan to the future: "Believe this, and you will have a home in heaven."

The past is in focus. The future is in focus. But panning from the past to the future makes a blur of the present. You get pushed out into the river with the depressing advice, "Follow the rules. Do the best you can. If you mess up, God will forgive you."

A Once Upon a Time Gospel can tell you something about the past, including your own sins and shortcomings. It can tell you something about the hope of heaven. But today, it leaves you to paddle upstream on your own.

A "Today" Gospel

The basic difference between a Once Upon a Time Gospel and a Today Gospel is *expectation*—expectation that Jesus Christ and the Holy Spirit are at hand, with particular plans for the expedition, here and now.

In chapter 3 we saw how Jesus promised His disciples that He would come to them and remain with them (John 14:28). He would be with them always (Matthew 28:20). He also promised that the Holy Spirit would come and be with them forever (John 14:17). *The kind of life you live as a Christian hinges on how you understand these promises.*

In terms of everyday life, many people take these words of Jesus in a poetic or symbolic sense, like the words of a dying friend who says, "I'll be with you, I'll always be with you." What they understand of course is that the friend will be with them in their *memory*. They will recall things that he said and did. They may even base important decisions on things he taught them. In that sense, he will be "with them."

This is how some Christians live their everyday lives. They remember things that Jesus said and did. They believe in Him. They try to live according to His teaching or teaching they associate with Him. That is how their faith plays out in everyday experience.

The words "faith" and "believe" deserve some scrutiny. If you were to walk down the street and randomly ask ten people, "Do you believe in God?" what kind of response would you get? Eight of them would give you a quick "Yes." Seven of them would mean by that, "Yes, I believe there is a God." For most people, believing in God means believing that God exists.

This falls far short of the biblical meaning of *faith*. No name in the last five hundred years is more strongly linked to the biblical idea of faith than that of Martin Luther. More than any other single individual, he was responsible for recovering the biblical teaching of "justification by faith." His understanding of faith went beyond an idea that you carry around in your head that you believe to be true. For Luther, the biblical idea of faith pointed to a *personal life-union between the believer and Jesus Christ*: "Faith, if it be true faith, is a sure trust and confidence of the heart, and a firm consent whereby Christ is apprehended: so that Christ is the object of faith. *Yea rather, He is not the object, but, as it were, in the faith itself Christ is present.*"[23]

This insight of Luther into the biblical meaning of faith has been underscored by the research of Tuomo Mannermaa and his colleagues in the "New Finnish School of Luther Research" at the University of Helsinki, Finland: When you "believe" in Christ it means that your life is dynamically united to Christ's life. You are in union with Him. He indwells you.[24]

This is a first step for breathing life into a Once Upon a Time Gospel. Your understanding of faith takes on new vitality. The difference could be pinpointed something like this: You go beyond saying, "I have faith in Christ," and declare boldly, "I have Christ in faith!"

This at once gives new life to the Once Upon a Time Gospel itself, but it goes beyond that. When Jesus promised His disciples that He and the Holy Spirit would be with them, He did not mean that they would simply help the disciples remember Jesus or think about Him. He meant that they would be with them to help, encourage, and lead them in everyday life. They would be with the disciples the way one person is with another person, in actual fact.

And yet there *would* be a difference because His life went through a change. Through His death and resurrection, Jesus became "a life-giving Spirit" (1 Corinthians 15:45). He would no longer be with them as a flesh-and-blood person but now as a Spirit person.

Relationship With a Spirit Person

Our niece Martha was about three when she reported a simple and profound discovery to her grandmother. She pointed to a picture of Jesus on the wall and said, "That's Jesus. I say Hi to Him, but He doesn't say Hi back to me."[25] Her sister, Nancy, younger by a year, picked up the thought and declaimed at the table one day, "Je'thuth, Je'thuth, Je'thuth! Dat's all I hear 'round here, but He don't say nothin'!"

With the innocent candor of childhood, they put their finger on a pivotal mystery of the Christian faith: Christians have a personal relationship with Jesus, but Jesus does not behave like an ordinary person. He doesn't come around so I can see Him. He doesn't speak out loud to me. He doesn't write me letters. He doesn't call me on the telephone. A person is someone I can talk to and be with, but "He don't say nothin'!"

It is not that our nieces were skeptics. They were simply realistic. They heard Jesus being talked about as a person. In prayers they heard Jesus addressed as a person. So they expected Jesus to behave like a person.

As a child grows older, he accommodates his thinking to his experience: Jesus *was* a person on earth long ago; one day we *will* meet Him in heaven as a person; but in the meantime, "He don't say nothin'!" The personal relationship with Jesus alternates between looking backward and looking forward, but does not touch down in the here and now.

Many adults could confess the same puzzlement and frustration voiced by children. They know about Jesus. They believe in Him. Yet the experience of a present relationship is vague or lacking.

Why is it that many Christians cannot say simply and confidently that they have experienced guidance from the Lord? Many even protest piously that it is presumptuous to think that one can know the specific will of God. If a child were sent to the store by his father, he would say, as a matter of simple fact, "My Dad sent me." How many Christians can say that they are where they are, doing what they are doing, because God has so directed their life?

Theological textbooks and evangelical tracts are fond of distinctions like, "It isn't enough to know about Jesus. You must have a personal relationship with Him." What do we understand such a phrase to mean? A personal relationship implies encounter and exchange between persons.

Suppose a husband and wife have a long talk over the supper table. They do not come away from the table wondering whether they have spoken with one another. They are not plagued with uncertainty as to whether a personal encounter has actually taken place. Yet, for many Christians, the sense of personal relationship with Jesus is plagued with a sense of uncertainty and vagueness.

The problem is the one discovered by our young nieces: Jesus does not behave like an ordinary person. How can you have a personal relationship with someone who doesn't say Hi back to you?

My father-in-law was once traveling in Germany and needed directions to a certain town. He saw a Shell service station—a comfortably familiar sign—and stopped to inquire. He came back crestfallen to those waiting in the car and reported, "He can't talk." What he meant of course was, "The attendant can't speak English." In America, a Shell service station is a place where you can speak to an attendant and get clear directions. But in Germany, even though Shell attendants speak, "They can't talk." For all practical purposes, "They don't say nothin'!"

This is the experience of many Christians. They know the outward symbols of personal relationship—words like see, speak, know. But when they try to enter into the experience of these words in another realm, the realm of the Spirit, they come away disappointed and frustrated.

Of course, we can offer the standard theological tranquilizers prescribed for quieting this kind of rowdy realism: We see Him with the eyes of faith; He speaks to us in the Bible; we meet Him as we encounter human need; we know Him in our heart. All of this is true. But for many Christians this comes across as a pious dodge for "He can't talk." They may take the pill and quiet down, but their longing for a truly personal relationship with their Lord remains unsatisfied.

It is not enough merely to say we see Him with the eyes of faith, we hear Him speak in the Scripture, we encounter Him in our involvement with people, we know Him in the depth of our hearts. Just as it would not be helpful to tell the American, "You must speak to the Shell attendant in *German*"—if you do not also tell him *how* to speak some German.

You can enter into a fine conversation with German Shell attendants once you have learned their language. And we can enter into a dynamic personal relationship with God the Father, with Jesus Christ, and with the Holy Spirit if we are willing to learn how personal relationship is conducted *in the realm of the Spirit*. A person who is a Shell attendant in Germany does not speak like an American for the simple reason that he is a German person, not an American person. The Lord does not communicate with us like a human person for the reason that He is a Spirit person.

By His incarnation Jesus became a human person in the fullest sense. He also remains forever the Son of Man, as well as the Son of God (Daniel 7:13; Revelation 1:13). The point here is that He now relates to us as a Spirit person. Thus the apostle Paul writes, "Even though we knew Christ as a man, we do not know Him like that any longer" (2 Corinthians 5:16, Phillips).

This is a simple fact, yet everything we are considering in this book hinges on it. Jesus said, "God is spirit, and his worshipers must worship in spirit and in truth" (John 4:24). This fact must occupy a more prominent place in our thinking when we speak about a personal relationship with God. The kind of relationship you have with a Spirit person is different from the kind of relationship you have with human persons.

Evangelical Christians speak warmly about a personal relationship with the Lord. The fact that this relationship is with a Spirit person is rarely mentioned. It rests, unexplained, on the analogy of a human relationship. People come away thinking that the characteristic of a genuine relationship with God is that it stirs thoughts, feelings, and imagination much like a relationship with a human person. The danger is that you begin to look too much within yourself for the authenticating marks of a relationship with God.

Of course we must use language or other appropriate symbols (pictures, actions, artifacts) in talking about a personal relationship with God. The danger is that one may become committed to the language of personal relationship without entering into the experience of it.

The danger here is subtle. An idea has a certain reality and existence of its own. We say that a person "holds an idea," but we also say that an idea "gets hold of a person." Most people carry on considerable inner dialogue with their own ideas. In a sense, we have a personal relationship with our own ideas. And this relationship with our own ideas has superficial similarities to a relationship with a Spirit person: intangibility, continuous availability, intimacy. The danger is that one may get an *idea* of a personal relationship with God, then enter into a relationship with the idea, thinking it is the real thing.

Our relationship with God will have certain similarities to other relationships. But in many respects it will be different, even frustratingly different. We must accommodate ourselves to manners of communication and modes of experience that are appropriate to a relationship with a Spirit person.

In chapter 6 we will give particular attention to how we experience Jesus Christ and the Holy Spirit, how They communicate with us and lead us in everyday life.

God supremely accommodated himself to the level of human

relationship in sending His Son to become a human being, the man Jesus. His purpose for the Incarnation was a means to an end—that we might become like Him (1 John 3:2).

While He was on earth, Jesus had a personal relationship with His followers as a human person. When His work on earth was finished and He prepared to return to the Father in heaven, He promised His disciples that the personal relationship would continue. But the nature of the relationship would change, for now it would no longer be with a human person, but with a Spirit person.

The initial response of the disciples was sadness. They could not imagine anything beyond the human relationship. Jesus' going away seemed to spell the end of their relationship with Him. But Jesus said, "It is for your good that I am going away. Unless I go away, the Counselor will not come to you; but if I go, I will send him to you" (John 16:7).

For His followers, Jesus foresaw not the severing of their personal relationship with Him, but a progression of that relationship into a new and more rewarding dimension. It is worth noting that after Jesus returned to the Father in heaven, He came again in spiritual presence to His disciples, with no trace among the disciples of hankering for the "good old days" when Jesus walked and talked with them as a human being on earth.

A young man leaves childhood behind—perhaps with a touch of nostalgia. But the adventure of entering into adult life soon absorbs him in a challenge and reality that goes beyond anything he knew in childhood. To return to childhood would be a retreat from reality. Just so, the disciples progressed from the reality of a relationship with Jesus as a human person into the greater and wider-ranging reality of a relationship with Jesus as a Spirit person.

When we Ride the River of God's will for our life, we do not merely *remember* Jesus Christ and the Holy Spirit. We are under Their day-by-day leadership. They are truly present to guide us, direct us, encourage us, comfort us, and help us in carrying out the Father's will and purpose. The fact that it is a *different* kind of relationship does not mean that it is any the less an absolutely *real* relationship.

Moving from a Once Upon a Time Gospel to a TODAY Gospel

The line between a Once Upon a Time Gospel and a Today Gospel is not hard and fast. More often it is a matter of gradation, moving from a lower level of expectancy to a higher level, consciously looking for the action of God in more and more areas of life.

The thing that jolted me out of my dogmatic slumber in a Once Upon a Time Gospel was the testimony of an Episcopalian minister's wife who prayed for sick people and saw them get well.[26] I had limited God's active intervention to the safe sanctuary of the past and to the equally safe sanctuary of my private inner life. A theologian might say that I had "dispensationalized Him into the past and subjectivized him into the psyche." With those two gates swung shut, I paddled the river pretty much on my own.

Then Jesus Christ stepped out of the neat, naturalistic time-space box that I had built for Him and said, *I am no different now than I was then. Yes, I do things inside the believer—kindle faith, cleanse from sin. But that is not all I do. I still heal the sick (oh yes, through doctors, but otherwise also). I do miracles. I reveal knowledge and wisdom. I lead where there is no path. I speak through dreams or visions. I guide and warn. I mount defense and do battle against spiritual powers of darkness.*

When I was called as a pastor to serve a congregation in San Pedro, California, I began to speak and teach about such things as healing, divine guidance, miracles, and gifts of the Holy Spirit. It raised questions, caused some controversy. One evening we had a special meeting, where people could come together in an informal setting and discuss some of the questions that were troubling them. Years later, one comment from that meeting remains vivid in my memory. A woman said, "Pastor, it's *supernatural*, and that's what scares us."

Behind the idea of "supernatural" is a God who may intervene in our everyday lives. That can be frightening, but it can also be exhilarating. Who wants a God that laid down a few guidelines in the Bible, then retired to a corner of the universe to watch us stumble along on our own?

Where will He lead? What will He ask of us? These are not questions that should frighten us or put us off. They should cause us to prick up our spiritual ears. God's plan for your life is a *good* plan. Jesus Christ and the Holy Spirit have a strategy for Riding the River that includes the stretch of river we are facing right now. Their leadership may call for innovation, adaptability; it may involve hardship. But it will advance us toward the goal that the Father wants us to reach.

Something as simple and biblical as praying for the sick required us to change our way of thinking, take on a new mind-set. Western culture is so steeped in the presuppositions of naturalism—everything has a natural, scientific explanation—that we cannot imagine God himself operating outside these boundaries. I cannot think of a more pointed way for the living God to shake up the thinking of people raised in Western culture than with a candid discussion of healing or miracles.

We had to move beyond the "scientific" thought world we were used to, because some of our people got hit with sickness, and the Spirit told us to "pray for each other so that you may be healed" (James 5:16). We did not always see healing take place, then other times we did. There is no formula for divine healing, or for anything else that the living God does.

Many things that people do in the world can be successfully copied—a good recipe, a scientific experiment, a computer program. Living the Christian life is different. Here we encounter the paradox of a God who is altogether *reliable*, yet altogether *unpredictable*. He is faithful. What He has promised, He will surely do. But *how* He will do it, we often do not know, or fail to recognize. We can easily overlook the testing and proving, the difficulty and hardship, that may be integral to His plan. He does what He himself has decided to do in the counsel of the Holy Trinity.

That is why the Christian life involves more than living by principles. Jesus did not intend His disciples to be guided simply by a commonsense understanding and application of spiritual principles. Not even the truths that He had taught them stood alone. He said, "I will pray the Father, and he will give you *another Counselor*. . . . He will teach you all things, and bring to your remembrance all that I have said to you" (John 14:16, 26 RSV).

One of the first lessons you have to learn when you Ride the River is that life on this expedition is not predictable. When you set out to follow God's plan for your life, be prepared to live with ambiguities, hardship, disappointments, and unanswered questions—but also with divine guidance, miracles, answered prayer, and, above all, the peace and joy of knowing your Captains' presence.

Jim Schmidt, a man in our congregation, made an astute observation: "If we were to pray regularly for the sick in the congregation, and five years go by with never once a healing, we would still have made a tremendous breakthrough. The very act of coming to God with such prayers breaks us free from the antisupernatural straitjacket of our scientific culture."

This was not a college dropout who wound up in a fundamentalist Bible school. He was a scientist himself, the lead engineer on the landing system of the Apollo moon shot.[27] Yet he was humble enough to recognize that there is a whole realm of reality that goes beyond the world of nature that a scientist explores, a realm that our culture has largely dismissed.

The faith gap between a Once Upon a Time Gospel and a Today Gospel needs to be dealt with. Believing in the Lord Jesus must go beyond knowing and accepting what He did two thousand years ago. It must be open to what He plans to do today. When you Ride the River, everything is keyed to the leadership of Jesus Christ and the Holy Spirit. You breakfast with them every morning, push out into the river, and proceed on.

Where faith in this kind of day-by-day leadership is weak or missing, it can be filled in.

Becoming Part of the Fellowship of Believers

In one sense, every believer has his own river to ride. Even before we are born, God has a specific life plan for each one of us. "All the days ordained for me were written in your book before one of them came to be. How precious to me are your thoughts, O God!" (Psalm 139:16–17). Yet no person Rides the River alone. We are signed on to be part of God's Corps of Discovery. Our personal life plan is linked to—dependent on—our being part of the fellowship of believers.

Every member of the Lewis and Clark Corps of Discovery knew that survival and success depended on sticking together. As resourceful and self-reliant as many of them were, no one thought of making the journey alone. Lewis and Clark's journals record how the whole Corps depended on the commitment and skill of the various members—the hunting prowess of George Drewyer; the courage and presence of mind of Sacagawea, who recovered the journals when they were washed overboard in a sudden squall; the prodigious strength of York, Clark's black servant; or the knack of John Shields for repairing rifles. They needed each other, and they knew it.

We need the fellowship and camaraderie of God's Corps of Discovery. The river can be a dangerous place if you are alone. The Father interweaves our life plans with the life and destiny of other believers. The leadership of our divine Captains includes the help, encouragement, correction, discernment, and balance that we receive from fellow believers—and the help they receive from us.

The help you receive from other believers may be as ordinary as a word of encouragement—"How good is a timely word!" (Proverbs 15:23)—or as practical as a fellow member coming by to help you repair a leak in your roof.

It may be more dramatic. When people in our congregation began to experience gifts of the Holy Spirit—particularly the gift of speaking in tongues—it caused some controversy. During a congregational meeting that had become quite contentious, Inga Horn, one of the elderly widows, whose family had helped found the congregation some years earlier, stood up and spoke a word of rebuke. A rebuke, under the anointing of the Spirit, is as different from mere human criticism as day is different from night. In her thick Norwegian accent she said, "What would *Jesus* say, if He was here and heard all this? These people have received something probably all of us should receive, and we're making all this fuss. We ought to be ashamed of ourselves!" The words were sharp, but no one took offense. The spirit in which Inga spoke was different than all the words that had been spoken before. The meeting ended. It took some months to work through questions and problems relating to charismatic renewal in the congregation, but the basic direction was clear: the gifts of the Holy Spirit would be welcomed in this congregation.

From the Day of Pentecost—when three thousand new believers were added to the company of the apostles—the Lord Jesus and the Holy Spirit have continued to exercise Their leadership in and through the fellowship of believers. If this link is absent or weak in your life, it can be made up. Exactly *where* you or your family maintain fellowship with other believers may involve specific guidance from God; some of the material in subsequent chapters may speak to such situations.

◎ Receiving the Holy Spirit

In his classic devotional study on the Holy Spirit, *The Spirit of Christ*, Scottish Presbyterian missionary Andrew Murray sees receiving the Spirit as a key step in a person's coming to faith: "The distinctive glory of the dispensation of the Spirit is His Divine personal indwelling in the heart of the believer . . . but He is received and possessed only as far as the faith of the believer reaches."[28]

Of course the Holy Spirit may do many things in a person's life before He is "received" in the New Testament sense. The Spirit is active in every aspect of a person's journey of faith. He may work powerfully in a person's life and ministry, as He did with some of Jesus' disciples before Jesus baptized them with the Holy Spirit on the Day of Pentecost. Seventy-two of them once returned from a brief mission "with joy and said [to Jesus], 'Lord, even the demons submit to us in your name!' " (Luke 10:17). In promising the apostles that they would receive the Holy Spirit, Jesus recognized that they already knew something of the Spirit's presence, yet He pointed them to what I would call a deeper level of intimacy: "You know him, for he lives with you and will be in you" (John 14:17).

David Pawson makes the point, "We must not assume that the Holy Spirit is a complete stranger before he is 'received.' It is His task to convict people of sin, righteousness and judgment, leading to repentance and faith. But all this can happen without a full awareness of His person, even while benefiting from His work."[29]

When we receive the Holy Spirit, we become more aware of Him as an actual presence in our life, a distinct *person*, just as Jesus promised.

According to the biblical pattern, receiving the Holy Spirit is one of the links that draws a person into the life of discipleship. It is as distinct and necessary as repentance, believing in the Lord Jesus, baptism in water, and becoming part of the fellowship of believers. *If it is missing in a person's experience, it can be made up.*

Helping People Receive the Holy Spirit

If you had never been baptized in water, you would present yourself as a candidate to someone who baptizes, usually the pastor of a church. If you have not yet received the Holy Spirit in the way that the Bible presents this experience, what you do is just as simple and straightforward: you present yourself to the One who baptizes with the Holy Spirit, the Lord Jesus. "The promise is for you . . . for all whom the Lord our God will call" (Acts 2:39).

In the Bible, the five links in the discipleship chain are strongly connected, yet each link remains distinct. According to the biblical pattern, receiving the Holy Spirit often comes near the end of the chain, though this is not always the case. If you want to receive the

Holy Spirit, it is well to make sure that other links are clearly in place: repentance toward God, faith in the Lord Jesus, baptism in water, and being part of the fellowship of believers. Then you can come to the Lord Jesus and ask Him to baptize you with the Holy Spirit.

Jesus linked the gift of the Holy Spirit to persevering in prayer: "Ask and it will be given to you; seek and you will find; knock and the door will be opened to you. For everyone who asks receives; he who seeks finds; and to him who knocks, the door will be opened. Which of you fathers, if your son asks for a fish, will give him a snake instead? Of if he asks for an egg, will give him a scorpion? If you then, though you are evil, know how to give good gifts to your children, how much more will your Father in heaven give the Holy Spirit to those who ask him!" (Luke 11:9–13).

Often it helps when other people who have received the Holy Spirit pray with you. Sometimes a pastor or other leader will lay hands on persons and pray for them to receive the gift of the Holy Spirit. If a group of people are gathered, including some people who want to receive the gift of the Holy Spirit, the group may simply have a time of prayer, encouraging people to pray for themselves, to receive the Holy Spirit. Scripture prescribes no particular manner in which you must pray to receive the Holy Spirit.

Speaking in Tongues, a Sign of the Holy Spirit

In the Bible how did people know that they, or someone else, had received the Holy Spirit? David Pawson makes a careful study of every New Testament reference on the topic and concludes, "A person filled with the Holy Spirit bursts into 'prophesying' of some kind. Spontaneous speech was the sign which accompanied [the first] and all later receptions of the Spirit."[30] The book of Acts describes the spontaneous speech with phrases like "declaring the wonders of God" (2:11), "praising God" (10:46), and "prophesying" (19:6).

The spontaneous speech most commonly mentioned in the

book of Acts, in connection with receiving the Holy Spirit, is the phenomenon that has come to be known as *speaking in tongues*.

In helping people include in their Christian experience the link of "receiving the Holy Spirit," it makes sense to give some prominence to the gift of speaking in tongues.[31] People should expect something to happen when they receive the Holy Spirit. There is no simpler or more natural "happening" to expect than the one most commonly mentioned in the New Testament record: they will speak in tongues.

Speaking in tongues, while unusual to begin with, soon becomes a very natural part of a person's prayer life. It is the simplest of gifts to receive and use. As a "prayer language" it is a source of blessing in the ongoing life of a believer, a reminder of the Holy Spirit's indwelling presence.

Speaking in tongues challenges the monopoly of the human intellect over one's prayer life. Speaking in tongues was likely in the mind of the apostle Paul when he wrote, "We do not know what we ought to pray for, but the Spirit himself intercedes for us with groans that words cannot express. And he who searches our hearts knows the mind of the Spirit, because the Spirit intercedes for the saints in accordance with God's will" (Romans 8:26–27). Scholarly research has generally recognized this as a reference to the widespread experience of speaking in tongues in the early church.[32] In Paul's mind, it is the gift that fits into his experience of weakness; it is not a sign of spiritual accomplishment, but belongs to the beginning or onset of the life of discipleship.

To speak in tongues, you must quit speaking in any other language that you know, for you cannot speak two languages at once.[33] After you have come to the Lord with prayers and petitions in your native tongue, lapse into silence and resolve to speak not a syllable of any language you have learned. Focus your thoughts on Christ. Then simply lift up your voice and speak out confidently, in faith that the Lord will take the sound you give Him and shape it into a language. Take no particular thought for what you are saying; your mind is "unfruitful" during the exercise of this gift (1

Corinthians 14:14). As far as you are concerned, it will be just a series of sounds. The first syllables and words may sound strange to your ear. They may be halting and inarticulate. You may have the thought that you are just doing it yourself. But as you continue to speak in faith, "boldly, confidently, and with enthusiasm" (Acts 2:4, literal rendering), and as the lips and tongue begin to move more freely, the Spirit will shape for you a language of prayer and praise that will be beautiful to the ears of the Lord.

The initial hurdle to speaking in tongues, it seems, is simply this realization that you must speak. (Many people wait and wait for something to happen, not realizing that the Holy Spirit is waiting for them to speak out in faith.) Once this initial hurdle is cleared, however, you will find your spirit wonderfully released to worship the Lord as your tongue speaks this new language of worship.

Once a person has spoken in tongues, he may do so at will thereafter. Two "testings" of this gift seem almost universal, and a word concerning them may save those who are new in the gift some needless anxiety.

The first test usually comes almost at once: it is the temptation to think, *This is just me, speaking nonsense syllables*. This is a natural thought, for the interaction between the believer and the Holy Spirit is so subtle that it is hard to draw a clear line between my speaking and His prompting. The temptation, when this thought comes, is to draw back and deny the gift or to quit using it. Our ultimate confidence cannot be in the experience itself but in God's Word: He has spoken in the Scripture concerning this gift, and I have come to Him, my heavenly Father, to receive it. He has promised not to give me a stone when I ask for bread (Matthew 7:9). Therefore I can be confident that what I am speaking is truly His gift of a new tongue. As you continue to use the gift, you will pass through this test and come to the confidence that this gift will become to you all that Scripture promises.

The second test usually comes after one has exercised the gift for a time—perhaps a few weeks or months. The initial joy and enthusiasm that one had in the use of the gift begins to fade. You can still speak in tongues as fluently as ever, but it doesn't seem to be "doing" anything for you. It's just a hollow shell, with no inner content. The temptation is to let the gift fall into disuse. This is a temptation that you must resolutely resist. Every gift of God involves a stewardship of that gift. One who receives the gift of tongues must from the beginning take this stance: God has given me a gift that I will use to worship Him for the rest of my life.

There could be a good reason why God allows the initial enthusiasm to wane. He does not want our use of this gift to be grounded on the shifting sands of our own feelings but on the solid rock of His Word. I do not pray in tongues because it gives me a continual thrill but because His Word gives me specific promises concerning the exercise of this gift: I am edified, I communicate with God, I give thanks well (1 Corinthians 14:4, 2, 17). Regardless of what I feel or do not feel, the Bible tells me plainly that the exercise of this gift will have positive results. I believe the Word.

God wants us to grow to the point where we act according to faith rather than feelings. The great blessing of speaking in tongues is found in its regular and disciplined use over a long period—months and years—not in the passing emotion of a few prayer sessions. It is a tool of prayer that sharpens and improves itself with use.

Since people often first experience the gift of tongues in connection with receiving the Holy Spirit, it is a common testimony that the exercise of the gift serves as an encouraging reminder of the Spirit's indwelling presence and thus of His active leadership in your life journey. It can be an invaluable addition to your "prayer toolbox," enhancing your worship and adoration of God, as well as a practical aid in discerning the mind and will of God. Marilyn Hickey, widely known through her writings on the life of faith and prayer, has written that "nearly every successful thing I've ever done came to me as a revelation after praying in tongues."[34] This is one person's testimony of the blessing this gift has been in her own life.

The Bible says that one who speaks in a tongue "utters mysteries in the Spirit" (1 Corinthians 14:2 RSV). I would understand this to mean that the gift of tongues enables us to carry on the prayer-conversation with God in ways, and in regards, that go beyond the limited field of our own knowledge and understanding.

Some years ago a research team from the American Lutheran Church visited our congregation to study speaking in tongues, which some of our people had begun to experience. In connection with their research, they asked me to make a recording of my own speaking in tongues during my private devotions.

More than ten years later Dr. Paul Qualben, the psychiatrist who had been a member of the research team, gave a lecture at a Lutheran seminary, during which he played this tape. A guest professor at the seminary, and a longtime missionary in Israel, Risto Santala, was present and heard it. He obtained a copy of the tape and listened to it many times. He detected that it was a clearly spoken mixture of Hebrew and Aramaic, a hymn of praise cast in Old Testament bridal imagery. The final verse read:

> Thou has made the Exalted One as if cursed by God,
>   and I shall bless the Bride.
> The light of God your Messiah becomes wonderful,
>   He will answer, thus He saves.
> I shall bless the Bride with the strong latter rain
>   here when she is hearing.
> Lift up your hearts![35]

What struck me when I read his translation of words I had spoken in tongues was how different the ideas and imagery were from my normal prayers in English. It was not that the words were outlandish or obscure in meaning, just that they were quite different from my usual way of speaking or praying.

Speaking in tongues accords us the unusual privilege of speaking about things that go beyond the limit of our own knowledge and experience, things pertaining to the kingdom of God, in words and speech not of our own making but chosen by the Spirit.

As I have thought about this since, it has made me more humbly aware that the Holy Spirit, though He indwells me, is profoundly *beyond* me. " 'My thoughts are not your thoughts, neither are your ways my ways,' declares the Lord. 'As the heavens are higher than the earth, so are my ways higher than your ways and my thoughts than your thoughts' " (Isaiah 55:8–9).

The Holy Spirit has ways of thinking and acting that I know nothing about. Yet, paradoxically, He wants to lead me in His ways. He has plans that exceed any plans I might fashion on my own. Day by day I need to bow low before His presence and the Father's will, quiet the clamor of my own ideas and desires, and entreat Him, "What do you want to say to me? Where do you want to lead me?"

After asking this, I trust that He will rule and overrule this day as I go about the things that I do in everyday life. Much of life is ordinary, but trusting that I am proceeding under the leadership of Jesus Christ and the Holy Spirit fills the most humdrum day with purpose and meaning. (See appendix 3, "Extended Comment on Speaking in Tongues.")

Maintaining Life in the Spirit

Receiving the Holy Spirit is a good and necessary beginning. As you Ride the River, however, your relationship with the Holy Spirit must be maintained and deepened. We must continually live in, and act upon, the reality that our life is indwelt by the Holy Spirit.

This is as necessary as, and in some ways similar to, one's first receiving of the Spirit, as Andrew Murray took care to point out:

> The Holy Spirit is not given to us as a possession of which we have control and which we can use at our discretion. The Holy Spirit is given to us to be *our* Master and to have charge of *us*. It is not we who are to use Him; He must use us. . . . Our asking for His working must be as real and definite as if we were asking for Him for the first time. . . . When Jesus gave to those who believe in Him the promise of an ever-

springing fountain of ever-flowing streams, He spoke not of a single act of faith that was once and for all to make them the independent possessors of the blessing. But He spoke of a life of faith that, in never-ceasing receptivity, would always and only possess His gifts in living union with himself.[36]

Seeing and Appreciating God's Revelation of Himself in His Holy Spirit Identity

As God reveals truth to us, we become accountable for it. For example, the apostle Paul said that "before the law was given, sin was in the world. But sin is not taken into account when there is no law" (Romans 5:13). Once the law was given, God held man responsible for it. Similarly, God holds us accountable for His unfolding revelation concerning the persons of the Holy Trinity.

When Jesus came on the earthly scene, God said, "This is my Son, whom I love; with him I am well pleased. Listen to him!" (Matthew 17:5). His disciples could never again think of God the Father apart from His divine Son. On the Day of Pentecost, the Holy Spirit made His appearance. Jesus himself had been their Counselor; now the *other* Counselor had come. Jesus clearly wanted His disciples to know the Holy Spirit not only as a *power* but as a divine *person*, as He himself was a person. Pentecost is an unfailing reminder that we can never again think of the Father, or the Son, without also recognizing the divine person of the Holy Spirit.

Receiving the Holy Spirit often intensifies one's awareness of the persons of the Trinity. As an indwelling presence, the Holy Spirit makes not only himself known, but Christ and the Father as well. As indicated in the previous chapter, our attention may, from time to time, focus now on one person of the Trinity, now on another, according to God's purpose.

Some years ago, at a conference in Germany, the leader of an evangelistic movement prayed to receive the Holy Spirit. At the conclusion of the conference he said, "I have long known Jesus as my Savior and Lord. I have led many people to faith in Him. But in these days, for the first time in my life, I have been able to say from the heart, *Lieber Vater!* [Beloved Father]."[37] In receiving the Holy Spirit, he was drawn closer to the Father.

He was a recognized spiritual leader, a man of proven maturity. Neither he nor anyone else belittled what the Holy Spirit had done through his life over many years. Yet he came to this point in his life where, as he put it, "I know that I need something more." He humbly presented himself to Jesus, the Baptizer, and prayed to receive the Holy Spirit. *Something missing was made up.*

Receiving the Holy Spirit Honors Christ

It was said of Frank Laubach, the "apostle of literacy" and a great man of prayer, that he would sit down beside a person and, in his arrestingly deep bass voice, roll out the question of the apostle Paul, "Have you *received*?"

With loving boldness we need to confront people with that same question today. The wonder of the indwelling presence of the triune God comes to light and life when we receive the Holy Spirit. Scripture knows nothing of a pious muting or neglect of the truth concerning the Holy Spirit. It solemnly warns against the danger of speaking against, grieving, or quenching the Holy Spirit (Matthew 12:32; Ephesians 4:30; 1 Thessalonians 5:19).

Andrew Murray asks pointedly, "Does the Holy Spirit have the place in the Church which our Lord Jesus would want Him to have?"[38] As the Holy Spirit glorifies Christ, so Christ also honors the Spirit and expects us to do the same.

Asking to "receive" the Holy Spirit, as Scripture presents this truth, does not detract from what the Holy Spirit has already done in your life. Nor does it diminish the centrality of your faith in Jesus Christ. On the contrary, you receive the Holy Spirit *because of* your faith in Christ. Jesus Christ does not do foolish or unnecessary things, and Scripture is unmistakably clear: Jesus baptizes with the Holy Spirit (Acts 1:5, 2:38–39). It is His way of introducing us to the Co-Commander of our life journey. (See appendix 2, "Extended Comment on Receiving the Holy Spirit.")

CHAPTER FIVE

THE LETTER OF INSTRUCTION

The Bible reveals basic principles and direction for our life journey.
Biblical truth, however, is often paradoxical. The Holy Spirit must
show us how to apply it in concrete situations.

IN A LETTER dated June 20, 1803, President Jefferson outlined in considerable detail his instructions for the Voyage of Discovery. In subsequent correspondence with Lewis he made it unmistakably clear that his written instructions were to be considered authoritative for the conduct of the expedition. Every member of the Corps of Discovery knew when he signed on that his daily life, riding the river, would proceed according to the authority of the president's written word.

Jefferson's Letter of Instruction established not only the purpose of the expedition and basic direction it should follow but also included guidelines for situations they would encounter along the way.

For example, one of the expedition's most astonishing achievements was Lewis and Clark's favorable contact with the Indians they met. In his introduction to the Lewis and Clark journals, Bernard DeVoto writes, "In personal dealings with [Indians] they made no mistakes at all. In so much that at the critical points it is impossible to imagine a more successful outcome or a better way of achieving it. . . . They were obviously unawed and unafraid, but they were also obviously friendly and fair, scrupulously honest, interested, understanding, courteous, and respectful."[1]

This was no accident. Lewis and Clark followed the instructions in Jefferson's letter—that they were to approach the Indians they met in the friendliest, most conciliatory manner possible. These instructions were put to many a practical test, often under trying conditions. Even in the midst of a shootout with hostile Blackfoot warriors, Lewis forbade Drewyer to shoot one of the Indians who was moving away, "as the Indian did not appear to wish to kill us."

Jefferson's written instructions were indispensable. The degree to which the Corps of Discovery was able to maintain friendly relations with Indians proved to be one of the most necessary features of the entire expedition. The presence of Sacagawea in their party—a Shoshone Indian woman with a nursing infant—was a visible sign of peace as they came in contact with other Indian tribes. The evident respect of the captains for the Indian leaders they met, for their people and their customs, won them respect in return. At critical points, the progress of the party—sometimes its very survival—depended on the help they received from Indians. Had they not had and followed Jefferson's Letter of Instruction in this one regard alone, the expedition might have failed altogether.

The Authority of the Written Word

The authority of written Scripture characterized the Christian faith from its beginning—a legacy brought over from the Jewish faith. On one of his missionary journeys, the apostle Paul came to the city of Berea in Macedonia. As was his custom, he went to the Jewish synagogue to tell them about Christ. The book of Acts describes the people in Berea as having "noble character" because "they received the message with great eagerness *and examined the Scriptures* every day to see if what Paul said was true" (17:11). Scripture was their measuring rod for verifying truth.

The Bible is God's Letter of Instruction for our life journey, the written word against which we must measure everything we encounter and do. The success of our journey depends on the revelation that God has provided in Scripture.

The authority of God's Word is no optional or trifling matter. As Moses was about to die, he said to the people of Israel, "Take to heart all the words I have solemnly declared to you this day. . . . They are not just idle words for you—*they are your life*" (Deuteronomy 32:46–47). Scripture is the truth that we live by, our authoritative guidebook as we Ride the River. "All Scripture is God-breathed and is useful for teaching, rebuking, correcting and training in righteousness, so that the man of God may be thoroughly equipped for every good work" (2 Timothy 3:16–17).

The awesome authority of Scripture is one of the greatest blessings God has given, yet its very authority can pose a problem: *it can subtly displace the Holy Spirit*. With an authoritative Scripture at hand, the fleshly mind (human reason operating independently of the Holy Spirit) crowds in to take charge. This can lead to a truncated Trinity of "Father, Son, and Holy Scripture." The danger is real. We can be Christians who Ride the River with a Bible clutched firmly in hand, but with scant awareness of the living presence of the Holy Spirit.

How the Holy Spirit Uses Scripture

The Bible reveals basic principles and direction for the journey—truth that we must apply in concrete situations—as we Ride the River. Scripture, however, does not stand by itself. The Holy Spirit does not simply tuck a Bible in our baggage, push us out into the river, and wave us off with a cheery, "Just do what's written in the Book." That is not His way of leading. He "stands beside us" when we read and study God's Word, so He can show us how to apply it in specific situations.

Many Christians believe that the Bible is an infallible guide because it was *written* by the inspiration of God. No less important, however, is that it can only be rightly understood and applied when it is *read* under the leading of the Holy Spirit.

The reason for this becomes abundantly clear when we consider the nature of biblical truth.

The Paradoxical Nature of Biblical Truth

The alleged contradictions in the Bible never particularly bothered me until a friend attacked one of my heroes. "St. Paul was a hypocrite," he said.

The apostle Paul had long been one of my favorite people. I admired his integrity and zeal. When he became a believer in Christ, it was no halfway thing. He went all out. His teaching of the Christian faith is that rare blend of clarity and profound depth that can speak to the simplest believer, yet challenge the greatest intellect.

If my friend had disagreed with Paul, or said that he had funny ideas, or that he wasn't worth one's time and attention, I could have charged it off to my friend's ignorance: he did not know St. Paul. But . . . a *hypocrite?*

"Look what it says in Galatians," my friend said confidently. " 'If you receive circumcision, Christ will be of no advantage to you' " (Galatians 5:2 RSV).

"What's wrong with that?" I answered back. "Paul is pointing out the difference between Christianity and Judaism. You don't have to observe the Jewish law of circumcision to become a Christian."

"But look what he does in Acts. 'Paul wanted Timothy to accompany him; and he took him and circumcised him because of the Jews that were in those places' (Acts 16:3 RSV). What a hypocrite! Telling the Galatians that Christians shouldn't be circumcised, but then he slips off and circumcises Timothy because he doesn't want to offend the Jews."

It brought me up short. Was St. Paul a hypocrite? I pondered that for some time. It led me into one of the most exciting studies of Scripture that I have ever experienced.

Many Scriptures Seemingly Contradict One Another

The apostle Paul was no hypocrite. The two Bible texts that my friend pointed out illustrate a basic feature of Scripture that we find it threaded through the Bible: *God often frames His truth in opposites, or paradoxes.*

"Enter not into judgment with thy servant; for no man living is righteous before thee" (Psalm 143:2 RSV). *Don't judge me, God. I could never stand up to judgment under your scrutiny. No person can measure up to your standard of righteousness.* Good, solid, evangelical doctrine. We are sinners, every last one of us.

But then, "Judge me, O Lord, according to my righteousness and according to the integrity that is in me" (Psalm 7:8 RSV). *Go ahead and judge me, God. My righteousness and integrity are up to it!*

You don't need a degree in theology to recognize a contrast between these two Scriptures, which is more than superficial. Theologically, they contradict each other.

The Lord once spoke about King Saul to the prophet Samuel: "I repent that I have made Saul king." The Lord was about to set Saul aside as king of Israel. A few verses later, however, we read, "The Glory of Israel will not lie or repent; for he is not a man, that he should repent" (1 Samuel 15:11, 29). God no sooner says, "I repent," than His inspired prophet says that God cannot repent. How do you handle that?

Of course these texts come from the Old Testament. The New Testament is different . . . isn't it? At least the words and teachings of Jesus?

Jesus said, "Heal the sick, raise the dead, cleanse lepers, cast out demons. *You received without paying, give without pay.*" Yet, in the very next verse, Jesus says, "Take no gold, nor silver, nor copper in your belts . . . *for the laborer deserves his food*" (Matthew 10:8–9 RSV).

What did Jesus mean? That His disciples should accept no pay for their services? Or that they should get something, at least their meals? It is not easy to tell, if you take the words in their plain sense. And this is not one of the most difficult texts by far.

These are simply examples, and not very important ones at that. But they point to a reality. From one end of the Bible to the other we find Scriptures that seemingly contradict one another. It is no accident. It is the very nature of applied biblical truth. "True wisdom has two sides" (Job 11:6).

An understanding of biblical paradox is a key to helping us find, and follow, the will of God as we Ride the River.

Life Itself Is Full of Seeming Contradictions

Paradox is nothing new or strange. We may not give it much thought, but we live with it every day. Language abounds with contradictory slogans that distill basic truths of human experience—

- Look before you leap.
- He who hesitates is lost.

On the face of it, these axioms are contradictory; they stand in paradoxical relation to one another. Which of these truths do you apply when you face a real–life situation?

On a June morning in 1805, Reuben Fields, one of the Corps of Discovery, was hunting for game. He spotted two grizzly bears. Creeping closer to get a shot at them, he stumbled on a third grizzly, which "immediately made at him being only a few steps distant." Fields ran for his life. He came to a steep bank above the Missouri River. Below lay a stony bar.

If the grizzly had been two minutes behind him, "look before you leap" might have made sense. Maybe he could have found a footpath, a safer way down to the river. But the bear was right at his heels.

Fields leaped down the steep bank, landing on the stony bar. He cut his hand, bruised his knees, and bent his gun. Fortunately the bank hid him from the bear, and he escaped.

Clearly, the truth for Fields in that situation was "he who hesitates is lost."

This is commonsense thinking, yet it goes to the heart of how we handle paradoxical truth in everyday life. According to the circumstance, you apply one pole of the paradox or the other. You cannot, in the same moment, both look before you leap and act without hesitation.

My wife, Nordis, accurately described the essential character of a charismatic awakening that occurred in our congregation in the early 1960s. She said that the Lord gave us two themes or desires:

- a deep, earnest desire to be faithful to the gift of the Holy Spirit and to the revelation and teaching we received;
- a deep, earnest desire that this renewal be a blessing in the Lutheran church (which we loved) and not cause trouble or discord.

These two things often stood in tension, opposing each other! That is the nature of paradoxical truths. They challenge one another; they do not harmonize with one another.

When I was a child, the first thing that greeted my eyes when my family visited our grandparents was the big grandfather clock standing in the living room, its long pendulum swinging gently back and forth. As long as the pendulum was swinging, we knew the time was accurate. If we came in and saw the pendulum stopped at dead center—a perfect compromise between the left arc and the right arc—we knew the clock was no longer functioning. It might be an interesting decoration, a conversation piece, but it couldn't tell you the time of day.

The "solution" to a paradox is not a compromise. You do not search for a point of balance halfway between the two poles of truth. The phrase favored by some theologians, "holding truth in tension," is equally unsatisfactory. Both of these formulas seek to resolve paradox at the level of abstract understanding.

True paradox is never resolved with the intellect. At the level of human understanding, the two poles of a paradox stare across the divide at one another in unyielding contradiction.

G. K. Chesterton made the point that Christianity keeps the

two poles of a paradox side by side, like two strong colors, red and white. "It has always had a healthy hatred of pink, the combination of two colors which is the feeble expedient of the philosophers. Christianity keeps the two colors co-existent but pure."[2]

The resolution of a paradox comes not in thought, but in life. You cultivate a mind-set that is prepared to *move in alternating rhythm between the two poles*.

Learning to Live With the Paradoxes in the Bible

The caustic secularist will say, "The Bible is a pack of contradictions. One writer wrote one thing, another wrote something else. They contradict each other all over the place."

This does not get at the real issue. The problem is not that in the New Testament an apostle wrote one thing, whereas in the Old Testament one of the prophets wrote something quite different; or that two apostles contradict each other; or even that the same person wrote one thing in one place and something contradictory in another.

What we are dealing with is a fundamental characteristic of God's Word. The presentation of truth through opposites is threaded into the warp and woof of Scripture. Getting a grip on the paradoxical nature of biblical truth opens up the Bible in new and down-to-earth ways.

A Scripture that illustrates this vividly—not without a touch of humor—is found in two consecutive verses of Proverbs. It is my candidate for Scripture's Perfect Paradox:

> Answer not a fool according to his folly, lest you be like him yourself. (Proverbs 26:4)
> Answer a fool according to his folly, lest he be wise in his own eyes. (Proverbs 26:5)

Well now, what should you do when you meet a fool—answer him back, or give him the silent treatment?

When King David fled Jerusalem during the rebellion of his son Absalom, a man called Shimei cursed him, threw stones at him, and charged him with the blood of King Saul, though in fact David had steadfastly refused to lift his hand against Saul. David's soldiers wanted to kill this man who was raving like a fool, but David restrained them. He accepted the man's curses without retort. In this situation, he "answered not a fool" (see 2 Samuel 16:5–12).

Earlier in David's life, a giant named Goliath spoke foolish words to him:

> He said to David, "Am I a dog that you come at me with sticks?" And the Philistine cursed David by his gods. "Come here," he said, "and I'll give your flesh to the birds of the air and to the beasts of the field."
>
> David said to the Philistine, "You come against me with a sword and spear and javelin, but I come against you in the name of the Lord Almighty, the God of the armies of Israel, whom you have defied. This day the Lord will hand you over to me, and I'll strike you down, and cut off your head. Today I will give the carcasses of the Philistine army to the birds of the air and the beasts of the earth, and the whole world will know that there is a God in Israel. All those gathered here will know that it is not by sword or spear that the Lord saves; for the battle is the Lord's and he will give all of you into our hands."
>
> As the Philistine moved closer to attack him, David ran quickly toward the battle line to meet him. Reaching into his bag and taking out a stone, he slung it and struck the Philistine on the forehead. The stone sank into his forehead, and he fell facedown on the ground. So David triumphed over the Philistine with a sling and a stone; without a sword in his hand he struck down the Philistine and killed him. (1 Samuel 17:43–50)

In this situation, David did not let the foolish boasts of the Philistine go unchallenged. He "answered a fool" first with words, then with deeds.

Clearly, in these two events, David was guided by a sense of the Lord's purpose in each of the situations. When one of his soldiers wanted to strike down Shimei, David said, "Leave him alone; let him curse, for the Lord has told him to" (2 Samuel 16:11). In the other event, he dared to go up against a giant because he had come to a firm belief that "the Lord . . . will deliver me from the hand of this Philistine" (1 Samuel 17:37).

It requires more than common sense to solve the paradoxes of Scripture; nor can they be smoothed over with mental trickery. They stare out at us from the pages of the Bible in all their truth and in all their contradiction. They frustrate the mind, which does not live comfortably with contradiction. They paralyze the will, which prefers to live by simplistic, unvarying formulas. But for the Spirit-led believer, they become God's NOW word—the particular truth of Scripture that God wants to apply in this situation.

It is important to note that paradoxical truth does not argue against biblical absolutes. Paradoxical truth has a different function, which is to *apply* truth in practical situations. Behind every biblical paradox stands one or more biblical absolutes.

For example, Jesus said to His disciples, "You will receive power when the Holy Spirit comes on you; and you will be my witnesses" (Acts 1:8). A Christian is, by the simplest definition, a witness for Jesus. Our lives are meant to bring honor to Him and draw other people to Him. The prayer "Lord, make me a witness" is never wrong or inappropriate.

But how do you do this? How do you live as a witness for Jesus in the circumstances of everyday life? When your friend cheats you in business? When you hear that your next door neighbor has been diagnosed with terminal cancer? When your teenage son is picked up by the police for drug possession? When you plan your family budget?

In any of these events you might come up with a Scripture that would seem to speak to your situation. The point is, if you looked a little longer, you could probably come up with another Scripture that would also speak to the situation, but would say something different, perhaps altogether different. Paradoxical truth cannot be applied according to some principle or rule of thumb. It requires the leading of the Holy Spirit.

Scripture brings out the distinction between absolute truth and applied truth by its use of two different terms. The distinction is obscured in translation because the same English word is used to translate both of the Greek terms: the Greek terms *logos* and *rhema* are both translated into English as *word*.

Karl Barth, the famous Swiss Reformed theologian, explained that *logos* is the Word of God that is *universal*. *Logos* states a general truth, a principle, or the inner content of an utterance. For instance, "God was in Christ reconciling the world to Himself, not imputing their trespasses to them, and has committed to us the [*logos*] of reconciliation" (2 Corinthians 5:19 NKJV).

Rhema, by contrast, refers to specific words directed to specific people. It is not simply truth that exists as a principle, but truth that is being applied to people's lives. *Rhema* is a truth that has been formulated into words and spoken in a given situation. It has a particular purpose in view, a purpose assigned by the Spirit.

Between the covers of the Bible we find a comprehensive digest of truth, a multifaceted *logos*. But in order for any part of that to become a *rhema*, it must be directed to a particular individual in a particular situation.

Many expressions of truth in the New Testament rest on the word *rhema*: "Man shall not live by bread alone, but by every [*rhema*] that proceeds from the mouth of God" (Matthew 4:4 NKJV). Jesus spoke this word from a verse in the Old Testament (Deuteronomy 8:3) to the devil during His temptation in the wilderness. He did not grab the verse at random. He received it for this particular circumstance.

The truth that we live by is not simply truth that is printed between the covers of the Bible. By itself, the Bible is like food in a refrigerator, waiting for the time when it will be prepared and eaten. It does not give life until the Holy Spirit singles out a particular truth and applies it to our lives. This is one of the distinctions between *logos* and *rhema*. Again, *logos* is used to state a general truth. *Rhema* refers to specific words directed to specific people. It is not simply a truth that exists as a principle. It is a truth that is formulated into words and spoken. It is this *act of speaking* that is particularly in view when the Bible uses *rhema*. And this is the truth that communicates *life*.

What we are calling a NOW word of God corresponds to Scripture's use of the word *rhema*.

Paradox and the Leading of the Holy Spirit

A police chief told me about a telephone call he had received one day. "You have to come and pick up my son," said a distraught father. "I can't do anything with him. Today I caught him smoking marijuana in his room. That's an offense, isn't it?" The chief affirmed that it was indeed an offense. "Well, come and get him. I can't do anything with him."

The chief began to talk with the man. "He's your son. How old is he?"

"Ten years old."

"Tell me a little bit about him," the chief said. The father declaimed again that he could not handle the boy. Nothing he said made a dent—the boy was incorrigible. As he described some of the things the boy had done, the chief ventured the thought, "Have you ever given him a spanking?"

The father paused a moment. "No," he said. "You mean I can do that?"

"There's no law against it."

"Just a minute, officer," the father said. The phone clanged down. The chief heard some talking in the background. After several minutes the father came back on the line. "Thank you, officer," he said. "I think you may have solved my problem."

The man called a month later to report that his son was "a new boy. We're talking and laughing and doing things together.

Our family is back on track again," the father reported enthusiastically.

It is true, of course, that the Bible says, "He who spares the rod hates his son, but he who loves him is diligent to discipline him" (Proverbs 13:24 RSV).

But what about love and understanding? What about the Prodigal Son! What about forgiveness?

My father told me an interesting story some years ago. He was the director of a summer camp for underprivileged children. When he first came on the job, he was handed a note from the man who had been camp director the previous summer. The message was brief and to the point: "Don't waste any time on Harvey Engman. He's hopeless. He ran away from camp three times last summer. He's nothing but a troublemaker."

My father went down to meet the train that was bringing the children to camp. They filed off and huddled together on the platform. Some of the little ones were uncertain and apprehensive, out of the city and away from home for the first time in their lives.

One of the bigger boys, thumbs hooked in his belt, elbowed his way to the front of the group. He glared at my father but said nothing.

My father told the children to stay on the platform until their baggage was loaded on a truck. Then, he said, they would walk in a group to the camp, about a half mile down the railroad track.

He turned around to speak to the truck driver. When he turned back, he saw the big boy taking off down the railroad track by himself, thumbs still hooked in his belt. *That'll be Engman*, my father thought. He decided to let the matter pass.

A little while later my father was resting in his cabin. A loud knock sounded at the door. He went to the door and opened it. There stood Harvey Engman, thumbs securely hooked into his wide brown belt, his head tilted to one side, jaw outthrust, daring anyone to take a swing at him.

"When's lunch?" he demanded.

My father told him that it would be ready in about twenty minutes.

"Well, shake it up!"

My father, though he was a quiet and gentle man, was a firm disciplinarian. His natural instinct was to take the boy by the collar and settle the matter then and there. Something restrained him. As he thought about it later, he said, "I guess the Holy Spirit was trying to tell me something."

At lunch he explained to the campers that after the meal they would be dismissed to their dormitories for a quiet time, while the staff had lunch together and planned camp activities for the following day. They could read a book, write a letter, take a nap—whatever they wished, as long as they were quiet. No talking.

They went off to their dormitories. On the girls' side, complete silence. On the boys' side, pandemonium.

My father walked over to the boys' dormitory. He didn't have to wonder what had happened. On the first bed inside the door Harvey Engman rested on his haunches, fingers drumming on the imitation leather belt where his thumbs seemed permanently moored, defiance and challenge written all over his face. If I had been there, I could have told Harvey from personal experience that challenging my father was a losing proposition. But again, as my father told me years later, "Something restrained me."

"Some of you must not have understood," he said. He went over the instructions again, explaining that the staff needed a time when they could talk together and plan activities. "I think what we need is someone who can take charge in here and see that things stay quiet." He turned to Harvey and said, "Will you take charge in here?"

Harvey's face fell in disbelief. "Me?"

"Yes. Would you take charge and see that things are kept quiet?"

The boy glanced around the room. His right thumb pulled loose from his belt. He tapped it slowly to his chest and said, "Leave it to me."

The hour passed without a sound from the boys' dormitory. Later my father asked a couple of the boys what had happened.

"Nothing," they said. "Harvey lay back on his bed, so the rest of us did too."

A transformation took place in Harvey's life. He became the model camper. He tracked my father like a shadow during his nine weeks at camp. He did everything he was told to do. At the end of the season he was voted "best camper" by the other children. When he pulled his thumbs loose from his belt to accept the award, there were tears in his eyes.

His teachers in public school wrote my father to find out what in the world had happened to Harvey Engman. All he talked about was camp. He was a changed boy.

In Harvey's whole life, nobody had ever invested an iota of trust in him. My father's simple question, "Will you take charge?" knifed through at a moment when a twelve-year-old boy was still open to receive it. The Holy Spirit knew that it was the way to handle Harvey Engman in that situation—to extend mercy, to show trust.

This experience initiated a lifelong relationship between Harvey Engman and my parents. Harvey, still active in Christian work at 85, visited my wife and me shortly before his death, and recalled this story.

So which is the right way to discipline a rebellious boy? The man who called the police chief got one answer. For my father and Harvey Engman, the Holy Spirit had a very different strategy. Both answers are rooted in Scripture.

Principles Alone Are Not Enough

We may believe strongly in the authority of Scripture. This is important, but by itself it will not ensure that we know and follow God's will in everyday life. According to Scripture, God's will may rest now on one pole of a paradoxical truth, at another time on its opposite. To take hold of the wrong pole of a paradox in a particular situation can be as disastrous as acting on an untruth; it misses God's will in that situation.

Apart from the leading of the Holy Spirit, Scripture is not only dead but death-dealing. All too easily we can miss the NOW word of God. We may have a general grasp of biblical principles, but if we fail to discern how the Spirit wants to apply them in real-life situations, we can go badly astray. Time and again we will miss the will of God in everyday life. Jesus himself pointed out the critical difference between words the "flesh" might apply on its own and words that the Spirit chooses and applies to the lives of His disciples. "The Spirit gives life; the flesh counts for nothing. The words I have spoken to you are spirit and they are life" (John 6:63).

Jefferson's Letter of Instruction to Lewis and Clark said, "We value too much the lives of citizens to offer them to probable destruction." The size of the Corps of Discovery would be sufficient to stand up to individuals or small parties of Indians. If they met a superior force of hostile Indians, Jefferson's instructions told them to turn back. Yet he left the decision with the captains: "To your own discretion therefore must be left the degree of danger you may risk."

If some group threatened their progress, what should the Voyage of Discovery do—advance or retreat? Both options were included in the president's Letter of Instruction. In two tense confrontations, members of the Corps of Discovery saw their captains employ quite different strategies.

When warriors of the Teton Sioux tried to block their progress, Clark drew his sword and made a signal for the men in the boat to prepare for action. At this show of bravery, the Teton chief stepped in and ordered his young warriors away.

In the wake of the gunfight that Lewis and three men from the Corps of Discovery had with Blackfoot warriors who tried to steal their guns and horses, the Indians lit out for their home camp. Lewis knew that they would return with reinforcements. He ordered a bone-wearying ride to put distance between themselves and a superior force of the Blackfeet. They rode a hundred miles in twenty-three hours. After one brief rest, Lewis wrote, "I was so sore that I could scarcely stand, and the men complained of being in a similar condition. I told them that our own lives, as well as those of our friends and fellow travellers, depended on our exertions at this moment. They prepared the horses and we again resumed our march."

In these two situations (the only threatening confrontations that the Corps of Discovery faced during the entire expedition), the captains employed opposite strategies. Jefferson's Letter of Instruction had laid the groundwork for both. The wise leadership of the captains spelled the difference between proceeding on and potential disaster.

For Paradox, You Need . . . a Person

The Bible sketches a broad picture of the different, indeed paradoxical, situations that life presents—

> For everything there is a season, and a time for every matter under heaven:
> > a time to be born, and a time to die;
> > a time to plant, and a time to pluck up what is planted;
> > a time to kill, and a time to heal;
> > a time to break down, and a time to build up;
> > a time to weep, and a time to laugh;
> > a time to mourn, and a time to dance;
> > a time to cast away stones, and a time to gather stones together;
> > a time to embrace, and a time to refrain from embracing;
> > a time to seek, and a time to lose;
> > a time to keep, and a time to cast away;
> > a time to rend, and a time to sew;
> > a time to keep silence, and a time to speak;
> > a time to love, and a time to hate;
> > a time for war, and a time for peace.
>
> (Ecclesiastes 3:1–8 RSV)

If we move slowly through the panorama of life described here, we may recall times in our own lives when we took hold of one pole of a paradox, but in so doing lost sight of its opposite. Or, we may recognize a conviction that we now hold, and feel defensive or uncomfortable to see its opposite cited in Scripture.

"There is a time to love, and a time to hate." How often do we come to grips with "a time to hate" in our understanding or presentation of the gospel? The gospel is centered in the love of God. But if even something as central as love is applied in a one-sided way, we can miss God's will and purpose. We can lose sight of His hatred of evil and blunt our sensibility of His righteousness. The biblical meaning of *love* can degenerate into mere sentimentality.

D. G. Kehl, in his book *Spiritual Disciplines for the Christian Life*, points this out in regard to worship. In commenting on Jesus' words, "God is Spirit, and his worshipers must worship in spirit and in truth" (John 4:24), Kehl says: "We worship God as He is revealed in the Bible, not as we might want Him to be. We worship Him as a God of both mercy and justice, of love and wrath, a God who both welcomes into Heaven and condemns into hell. We are to worship in response to truth. If we don't we worship in vain."[3]

"A time to love, and a time to hate." How do we know when either time is at hand?

Another example: "A time to keep silence, and a time to speak." Bill Bright, founder of Campus Crusade for Christ, said that he often tests the water to see whether it is a time to speak or a time to keep silent. He once stepped into an elevator that had an operator. He ventured some conversation. "Up and down, up and down, all day long."

"Yep," the man agreed cheerily, "that's the story of my life."

Bill tested the water. "Someday you're going to go up and keep right on going—if you're ready. Are you ready?"

The man said, "I don't think I am."

"Would you like to know how to get ready?"

"Yes, I would," the man said in all seriousness.

Bill shared the gospel with him and prayed with him. Bill's comment was telling: "If he had said, 'What are you—some kind of a religious nut?' I would have shrugged my shoulders, wished him good day, and gone on my way."[4]

"A time to keep silence, and a time to speak." How do we know when either time is at hand?

There is no "principle" that can tell us which pole of a biblical paradox to apply in a particular situation. Nor can we simply fall back on common sense. When Jesus explained to His disciples that "he must go to Jerusalem and suffer many things at the hands of the elders, chief priests and teachers of the law, and that he must be killed and on the third day be raised to life" (Matthew 16:21), He was speaking very *uncommon* sense.

The very fact that the Bible sets paradoxical truths before us underscores our need for the active leadership of Jesus Christ and the Holy Spirit. You cannot deal with paradoxical truth by means of a principle: you need a divine *person*. When you Ride the River, the primary question is not how much you know, but whom you are following.

A strong belief in the authority of Scripture must be wed to an equally strong faith in divine guidance. That is the choice we make when we Ride the River. We accept the present, active leadership of Jesus Christ and the Holy Spirit for our life journey. They guide us in the practical application of Scripture, helping us discern where God's pendulum of truth is swinging in the situation we presently face.

CHAPTER SIX

HEARING AND HEEDING
THE CAPTAINS

*As we Ride the River of God's empowering presence, Jesus Christ
and the Holy Spirit reveal their plans in a variety of ways.*

PRESIDENT JEFFERSON set forth the basic purpose and direction
for the Voyage of Discovery in his Letter of Instruction, leaving to
the discretion of Lewis and Clark how to apply his instructions in
specific situations.

As the journey got under way, ordinary aspects of daily life fell
into a routine—preparing meals, breaking camp, dragging canoes
across sandbars, singing and dancing around the evening campfire.
The men applied their knowledge, skill, and growing understanding of their captains in carrying out the ordinary chores of the
journey. Yet the reality of the unknown or unexpected lay always
close at hand. Day after day the direction and success of the
expedition depended on the active leadership of Lewis and Clark.
For members of the Corps of Discovery this meant being habitu-
ally on the alert to hear, understand, and follow specific commands that their captains would give them.

The Inner Witness of the Holy Spirit

Although divine guidance grows out of the Lord's real and
continual indwelling presence, this does not mean that we expe-

rience a continual stream of revelation concerning every aspect of life. The Lord leaves to our knowledge and judgment—sometimes even to our preference—many things that pertain to the ordinary routines of daily life.

Ted Hegre, founding president of Bethany Fellowship in Minneapolis, told how he began to ask for the Lord's guidance in virtually every aspect of his life. "One morning," he said, "I stood before my closet door and asked, 'Lord, which tie should I wear?' And the Lord answered, 'Well, which tie do *you* like?' " Hegre related this to underscore the need for perspective and balance in our understanding of divine guidance. God calls us to be followers, not robots.

Nevertheless, in this chapter we want to consider how we come to hear, understand, and follow our divine Captains when they exercise active leadership in our lives. To put it another way, we want better to recognize, and act upon, *the inner witness of the Holy Spirit.*

This phrase, "the inner witness of the Holy Spirit," provokes divergent impressions. At one extreme, any mention of an inner witness of the Holy Spirit is dismissed as a self-induced state of mind. At the other extreme, virtually any impression is accepted uncritically as the inner witness of the Holy Spirit.

We are thankful that we met the wonderfully wise old Pentecostal Bible teacher, John Wright Follette, in the early 1960s. His favorite text was, "Let us leave the elementary teachings about Christ and go on to maturity" (Hebrews 6:1). With wry good humor he would caution the immature and enthusiastic: "Settle down, now, or you're liable to fall out of your highchairs."

We need to consider how to understand and respond to a *genuine* inner witness of the Holy Spirit.

What happens if you are sitting in a tent by yourself, the flap opens, and another person steps in and says something to you? You look up. You see the other person. You hear him speak. You likely enter into conversation with him.

True enough, your brain registers the event. You have an

awareness within yourself—an "inner witness"—of the person's presence. The reason for this is not mysterious or merely subjective. It is caused by the objective presence of the other person who stepped through the flap of your tent.

That which stands behind a genuine inner witness of the Holy Spirit is awesomely objective: *it is the living presence of the Holy Spirit himself.* Of course, we do not discern the presence of the Spirit with our physical senses or with scientific instruments, the way we recognize something on the plane of physical reality, but through *faith.* The source of a genuine inner witness of the Holy Spirit is the presence of the Spirit, apprehended by faith.

Two Dangers

The inner witness of the Holy Spirit presents us with two equal and opposite dangers.

One danger would be to act on presumption, rather than faith, mistaking mere feeling, wish, or inclination for the inner witness of the Holy Spirit. The Bible tells us, "We know in part and we prophesy in part. . . . We see but a poor reflection as in a mirror" (1 Corinthians 13:9, 12). Our spiritual perception may not always be accurate.

The opposite danger would be to refuse to act, out of timidity, fearing that the inner witness of the Holy Spirit is not real, or that we may have perceived it inaccurately.

In chapter 5 we saw how the apostle Paul was forbidden by the Holy Spirit to go into Asia. He was then forbidden by the Spirit of Jesus to go to Bithynia, lying in the opposite direction. He and his companions ended up in Troas, on the coast, facing Macedonia (Acts 16:6–8).

How were they forbidden? The record does not go into detail. From other incidents in the book of Acts, however, we can infer that they came to a settled conviction that the Lord was so leading them; they had the inner witness of the Holy Spirit. They did not shrink from acting on their best sense of how the Lord was leading.

We need to be on guard against BOTH of these dangers, *presumption* and *timidity*.

Sometimes I have had to plead with people to consider at least the theoretical possibility that they may have heard the Holy Spirit inaccurately. That is not a put-down on them or their spirituality. It simply recognizes that we sometimes act according to what the Bible calls "the flesh."

It is a sign of spiritual growth when someone can say, quite matter-of-factly, "I guess I wasn't tuned in on that one; I didn't hear the Lord accurately." You draw back, pray again, seek counsel, reexamine Scripture, listen some more, and move ahead. It does not mean that you give up on divine guidance. It just means that you are open to correction. You recognize that sometimes you may perceive the Lord's will inaccurately or only partially.

The other side of it, however, is that, despite our weaknesses, Jesus Christ and the Holy Spirit continue to lead us in our everyday life. They are not at a loss to communicate with us in ways we can grasp. As the terrible toll of the American Civil War and the fateful decisions he had to make weighed on the shoulders of Abraham Lincoln, he expressed confidence in divine guidance: "I am satisfied that when the Almighty wants me to do or not to do a particular thing, he finds a way of letting me know it."[1]

Bob Whitaker, a Presbyterian pastor, was participating in a conference in South Africa. He told us about a man who came to one of his workshops, a black pastor from the bush. At home, the man had had a vision concerning this conference. In the vision he saw a particular building that he had never seen before, then a particular room in the building, then a particular chair in that room. He saw himself sitting on the chair, receiving a blessing. As he prayed about it, the pastor felt so moved by the vision that he traveled to the conference. He came to the site of the conference, a place he had never seen before. Suddenly he saw the very building he had seen in his vision. He went into the building and found the room he had seen in the vision, in which Bob Whitaker was conducting a workshop. He went to the chair he had seen in the vision and sat down. In the course of the workshop, Bob Whitaker prayed for him. The man received a tremendous anointing of the Spirit. He told Bob how the Lord had led him to the conference and to this particular workshop. He had an inner witness of the Holy Spirit, he followed it, and God met him.

Alongside an unusual testimony like that, it is well to recall the delightful story that well-known Bible teacher Bob Mumford told—just to remind ourselves that we are still in the flesh; we do not always hear the Lord accurately.

Bob was driving down a street one day, and he thought the Lord said to him, "Turn right on this next street, go down two blocks, turn left, and in the third house on the right, the little one with the brickwork, there is a man ready to receive Christ. Go and witness to him." Bob had heard stories about people getting this kind of guidance. He turned to the right, drove down two blocks, turned left, drove to the third lot on the right—an empty lot. No little house with brickwork anywhere in sight. He shook his head and said, "I must not have heard correctly."

He laughed in telling about it. It did not dampen his belief in divine guidance. In many other situations he perceived the Lord's will accurately. He knew that God sometimes guides people by strong inner impressions; he had learned of this both in Scripture and in daily life. But he saw that the Lord wanted to teach him something: You can mistake a random thought for the leading of the Holy Spirit. It was no great loss; he spent a little time driving a few blocks. He learned the valuable lesson that his spiritual perception could be inaccurate.

Admitting mistakes in our attempts to hear God is crucial for the body of believers at large, particularly for those new in the faith. They need to see in us, and in our attempts to discern God's will, a spirit of honesty and humility. However, they need also to see that, through practice, we can learn to distinguish more accurately between God's voice and our own thoughts.

Lewis and Clark did not lay out a course in *Exploration 101* for the Corps of Discovery to memorize and put into practice. Instead, they taught by meeting challenges as they arose. For example, something as basic as the need to secure a daily supply of food presented no real problem, and therefore no unusual leadership decisions, until they came to the Bitterroot Mountains more than a year after the start of their journey. In the mountains they no longer found the plentiful supply of game they had grown used to on the prairie. They had to learn to survive on meager rations.

In this chapter we want to address the question of how the Lord communicates with us. The material is not laid out as an orderly or exhaustive set of principles for you to learn and put into practice. Instead, I share some of the things I have learned along the way in my life journey, some of the help and wisdom I have received from other people, some of the ways God has made His NOW word real and effective in practical situations. Think of it not as a textbook, but more as a travelogue or journal, a reminder that each new morning we push out into the river with divine Captains who know how to speak with us and lead us.

Two arenas command our attention when we think about receiving or hearing a NOW word of God: *the Bible* and *circumstances*.

The Lord Communicates With Us Through the Bible

In the previous chapter we saw how, in the Bible, the Father has given us His Letter of Instruction for our life journey. We saw that the Holy Spirit not only confirms the truth and authority of the written word, He also inspires us to understand it and put it into practice under His leadership.

In considering how Jesus Christ and the Holy Spirit communicate with us, three aspects of biblical truth deserve further mention:

• the role of prayer

- what Scripture says about guidance
- the exercise of spiritual gifts

Prayer

Undergirding everything in this chapter is the *life of prayer*. In our life journey, prayer is like gathering around the breakfast campfire, talking over the day's assignments. Sitting around the evening campfire, discussing the day's happenings. Going over plans for the next day or the next week. Pulling over to the shore to take care of an emergency that has come up. Prayer is the normal setting in which our day-by-day interchange with Jesus Christ and the Holy Spirit takes place. It is the two-way communication link between believers and the Lord. If we mean to follow Jesus Christ and the Holy Spirit, prayer will become a way of life.

The subject of prayer, and the list of books and helps on prayer, is huge. It goes beyond the scope of this book to present even a primer on prayer. Yet I want to emphasize the central position that prayer must occupy in any serious consideration of divine guidance. (See the bibliography for suggested books on prayer.)

What Does Scripture Say About Divine Guidance?

Can we, as a practical matter, actually know and follow God's plan in everyday life? This question raises an issue of personal faith.

Imagine a conversation that goes something like this: "Do you believe that God actually 'speaks' to people, makes himself known in understandable ways?"

"Oh, yes! He spoke to Moses. He spoke to the prophets. He spoke to Jesus and the apostles."

"But do you believe He will speak to *you*? Can you ask Him a personal question? Will He guide you in something you are facing in your own life right now?"

Suddenly, many of us are not so sure.

Some years ago I was speaking at a prayer retreat in a Lutheran church. We studied various kinds of prayer. I gave a teaching on what I had termed a "prayer of faith."

During the discussion, I said almost offhand, "If you don't know something is the will of God, don't pray for it." I wanted to make the point that you should back up a step and pray for guidance; find out what the will of God is, then pray with expectant faith.

One woman sent a shocked look back at me. "I can't presume to know the will of God," she said. "I may *hope* that what I pray for is the will of God, but I surely can't *know* that it is the will of God."

She put her finger on the first question we must ask if we want to think seriously about finding and following God's plan in everyday life. Does Jesus Christ speak to us? Will the Holy Spirit lead us? Or is the very idea a conceit, delusion, and presumption?

What does Scripture say?

We turn first to the book of Acts. Acts is not only a history of the early church, it is also an enduring example for the church in all times and places. It continues the Old Testament tradition of imbedding the revelation of God's will and purpose in events of "holy history." Israel's God was not the lofty, abstract, impersonal God of the philosophers. Israel's faith was in a God who intervened in their experience. A God high in heaven, yet a God come down to earth. A God active in history, carrying out His plan.

The faith of Israel was faith in "the God who led us out of Egypt." The faith of the apostles built upon that foundation, as they proclaimed their faith in "the God who raised Jesus from the dead." The faith of the early church continued in the same vein, as Christians told of their faith in "the God who poured out upon us the promised Holy Spirit, who dwells in us, even as our Lord Jesus foretold."

In the pages of Acts we see the early church live out and testify to this trinitarian faith. Acts shows us how rich and varied are the ways that believers experience the empowering presence of God in everyday life.

Once, when there was a controversy in the early church, the

leaders met together in Jerusalem. They discussed and debated the controversy for some time. Then they sent a letter to believers in Antioch, Syria, and Cilicia in which they gave a judgment on the matter in question. They described it this way: "It seemed good to the Holy Spirit and to us . . ." (Acts 15:6–29). After a thorough discussion among the apostles and elders, a consensus emerged that reflected the mind of the Holy Spirit. That was how God "spoke" in this particular situation, bringing them to a knowledge of His will.

Some years earlier, when they wanted to ask God how they should select a twelfth apostle to replace the traitor Judas, they drew straws (Acts 1:26 TLB). In that situation, they believed the person of God's choice would draw the long straw.

When Saul of Tarsus encountered the Lord Jesus on the road to Damascus, he heard a voice telling him to "get up and go into the city, and you will be told what you must do." Then a man named Ananias had a vision in which he was commanded to "go to the house of Judas on Straight Street and ask for a man from Tarsus named Saul" (Acts 9:6–11). These are yet other ways that God spoke to people in the early church, through a voice and through a vision.

Some years after Pentecost, Cornelius, an officer in the Roman army, had a vision of an angel who told him to send for a man called Peter. At the other end, God gave a vision to Peter telling him to respond to the invitation. The result of these two visions was that a group of Gentiles received the Holy Spirit and were baptized into the Christian community (Acts 10:1–48).

We have noted how the apostle Paul and his companions were kept by the Holy Spirit from preaching in the province of Asia and prevented by the Spirit of Jesus from entering Bithynia. They found themselves in a narrow corridor, prevented by the Holy Spirit from going south, not allowed by the Spirit of Jesus to go north. Ahead of them lay Troas, on the west coast of modern-day Turkey, facing Europe across the Aegean Sea. And there, "During the night Paul had a vision of a man of Macedonia standing and begging him, 'Come over to Macedonia and help us.' After Paul had seen the vision, we got ready at once to leave for Macedonia, concluding that God had called us to preach the gospel to them" (Acts 16:9–10).

Step by sure step this missionary team was led to take the gospel to Europe. We are not told precisely how they perceived or recognized divine guidance at each point along the way. Often it may have been simply a clear inner conviction, perhaps a sense of peace, as people sometimes experience God's leading today. Other times it was more dynamic—a vision, a dream, a prophetic word. In any case, Scripture leaves us in no doubt: behind every decision was the conviction that Jesus Christ and the Holy Spirit were leading them.

Toward the end of Acts, we see the apostle Paul as a prisoner on a ship headed for Rome. During a storm, an angel of God stood beside him and said, "Do not be afraid, Paul. You must stand trial before Caesar; and God has graciously given you the lives of all who sail with you." Paul, confident that the Lord had spoken to him, told the crew that no life would be lost, though the ship would run aground in the storm. It happened exactly as he said (Acts 27:21–44).

These examples from the life of the early church were selected almost at random. A further study of the New Testament would only confirm the truth that they illustrate: *in the life of the early church, God spoke to believers and led them in a variety of ways.*

Next we look at the broader context of Scripture. In being led by Jesus Christ and the Holy Spirit, the early church was living according to familiar promises in the Old Testament scriptures.

"He guides the humble in what is right and teaches them His way. All the ways of the Lord are loving and faithful for those who keep the demands of his covenant" (Psalm 25:9–10). God leads His covenant people to know and follow in His ways.

"Yea, thou art my rock and my fortress, for thy name's sake lead me and guide me" (Psalm 31:3). The psalmist identifies himself with the living God; he calls on God, confident of divine guidance.

"In your unfailing love you will lead the people you have redeemed" (Exodus 15:13). Days earlier this people had been slaves in Egypt. They escaped the pursuing chariots of the Egyptian pharaoh by a miracle, passing through the Red Sea on dry ground. In this line from the "Song of Moses," celebrating Israel's deliverance, they sang out their confidence that the God who had *redeemed* them would now *lead* them.

The history of God's people, both in the Old and the New Testament, forges an unbreakable link between redemption and divine guidance. Scripture testifies to it at every turn: the books of history, the Psalms, and the prophets in the Old Testament; the Gospels, the book of Acts, and the Epistles in the New Testament. *God guides those whom he redeems.* This is the foundation of our understanding and our faith when we pray for guidance.

We make a point of this not because it is a new or startling idea. It is a familiar biblical truth. Yet in our everyday life this truth is often riddled with unbelief. In practice we do not always live as though the God who spoke in the Bible will still speak today. We need to break free from unbelief that lowers our expectations to the level of our own experience—or *lack* of experience! We need to restore a biblical base to our thinking, rekindle faith in the active leadership of Jesus Christ and the Holy Spirit.

God guides those whom he redeems. This is the biblical truth that gives believers the courage and confidence to proceed on in their voyage of discovery.

The Bible warns against ignoring divine guidance. "Those who live according to the sinful nature have their minds set on what that nature desires; but those who live in accordance with the Spirit have their minds set on what the Spirit desires. The mind of sinful man is death, but the mind controlled by the Spirit is life and peace" (Romans 8:5–6).

In most Christian groups or congregations, open rebellion

against the authority of Jesus Christ and the Holy Spirit is not the problem. A more insidious problem pervades the Christian community: As believers, we often ignore the active leadership of Jesus Christ and the Holy Spirit. We do not take it seriously or understand how it works. We head upriver, perhaps even with great spiritual enthusiasm, but expect to follow our own reason, desires, or judgments.

It is a subtle kind of insubordination: making decisions—either doing something or neglecting to do something—without the Lord's say-so. The apostle Paul reproached the congregation in Corinth, "I could not speak to you as to spiritual people but as to carnal, as to babes in Christ" (1 Corinthians 3:1 NKJV). They had started the journey, but they were still carrying on like ordinary people, following their own impulses and desires.

The Bible calls it walking according to the flesh rather than according to the Spirit (Romans 8:4). "Walking according to the flesh" describes a life ruled by the self—your own opinions, will, and desires exert leadership. "Walking according to the Spirit" describes a life that yields leadership to the Spirit of God.

Andrew Murray identifies a self-led spirituality as the single greatest obstacle to making progress in the Christian life: "Satan has no more crafty device for keeping souls in bondage than inciting them to a religion in the flesh. He knows that the power of the flesh can never please God or conquer sin." In answer to those who ask why their best efforts so often end in failure and produce few lasting results, Murray says, "It is self doing what the Spirit alone can do; it is the soul [self] taking the lead, in the hope that the Spirit would second its efforts, instead of trusting the Holy Spirit to lead and do all, and then waiting on Him." The root of the problem is seeking to follow Jesus "without the denial of self."[2]

Scripture links guidance to growth. The apostle Paul told the congregation in Colossae that he was praying for them, "asking God to fill you with the knowledge of His will through all spiritual wisdom and understanding. And we pray this in order that you may live a life worthy of the Lord and may please Him in every way: bearing fruit in every good work, *growing in the knowledge of God*" (Colossians 1:9–10).

In principle, finding and following the plan of God is a simple matter of following Jesus Christ and the Holy Spirit. In practice, learning to know and follow the ways of the Spirit does not come automatically, or all at once. We do not readily give up our independent ways.

The men in the Corps of Discovery learned to trust Lewis and Clark by stages. As the expedition proceeded on, their leadership took hold with the men. Discipline continued, but the need for strong punishments tapered off, finally ceasing altogether by February 1805. A sense of camaraderie and *belonging* gradually displaced a regimen of rules and regulations as a motivating force.

In time, the relationship between the captains and the Corps of Discovery became as close and natural as a family. About fifteen months into the journey, Lewis noted in his journal, "Sergeant Gass lost my tomahawk in the thick brush and we were unable to find it. I regret the loss of this useful implement. However, accidents will happen in the best families." Like the wise leader he was, Lewis knew that forgiveness is central to the life of a family.

Day by day the men experienced an excellency of leadership that won their respect, confidence, and ungrudging obedience. If anyone could lead them to the Pacific Ocean and back again, it was their two captains.

The leadership of Jesus Christ and the Holy Spirit usually takes hold by stages, as we learn to listen to them and follow them in real-life situations. Concrete experiences of being led by the Spirit help permeate our thinking with the wisdom of God's ways.

In 1996 the Lutheran congregation in San Pedro, California, where I had earlier served as pastor, celebrated its seventy-fifth anniversary. One of the stories recounted during the celebration was an experience of divine guidance. It helped reshape the way that members, particularly those with leadership responsibility, approached making decisions in a Christian fellowship.

It had become evident that the congregation needed larger facilities to accommodate a growing youth program. Ninety grade-school children were crowded into a small parish hall every Wednesday evening. In addition, we had to borrow the facilities of a local synagogue in order to accommodate about forty teenagers.

For more than a year we talked and prayed about it. A few years earlier the congregation had experienced answered prayer in regard to finances. Seven men had met every week to pray for some projects that we felt we should undertake but for which we had no money. About thirteen thousand dollars came in, over and above the budget, and we were able to do some of the projects. What faced us now was much bigger. The building we needed would cost about a hundred thousand dollars—a large amount in the 1960s for a congregation of two hundred adult members.

By the spring of 1969 we felt that it was time to get started. We had two unresolved questions:

- When should we begin? A building-fund drive begun in the late spring would probably run into the summer. It might be wiser to wait until the fall, when people got back from vacations.
- How should we do it? The thought had come to us that maybe God wanted to do something altogether different. Maybe He wanted to "visit" people himself, in His own way. We would simply show the kind of building we needed, and then let people respond as God moved them: "We won't call you, you call us." It seemed a little extreme.

On a Friday morning in June, as I came into my study, I saw a large manila envelope lying on the floor below the mail slot. I opened it up. The first thing that caught my eye was a thousand-dollar bill. Then another, and another—five in all. And bundles of hundred-dollar bills. I dumped the contents of the envelope on my desk and counted out twenty-five thousand dollars in cash.

To this day, no one has the slightest idea where the money came from.

There was no identification on the envelope, only a Bible notation—*2 Corinthians 6*. A verse at the beginning and a verse at the end of that chapter seemed to speak to the questions we had been pondering.

When should we begin? "Behold, now is the accepted time."

How should we do it? "God said, 'I will dwell in them and walk among them. I will be their God, and they shall be My people' " (2 Corinthians 6:2, 16).

We had a thanksgiving service that evening for this unexpected gift. I said to Lou Hefner, one of the deacons, "We've been asking God what we should do and when we should begin. It looks like He's given us a nudge."

"Pastor," he responded, "that was no nudge. It was a swift kick in the pants!"

That afternoon, one of the women in the congregation had received a word of prophecy: "Many will give more than a thousand dollars."

After the service, Ella Castell, one of the widows in the congregation, came up to me. "I've been wondering when the building program was going to get under way, and it looks like it is now. Here is my gift." She handed me a check for a thousand dollars. It was the first of many such gifts.

We followed the leading, admittedly unusual, and quite beyond anything we had previously experienced. There was no formal fund-raising. We began to build before the full amount of money was in hand. The prayer continued. Sometimes gifts came in just a day or two before money was needed to meet a payment with the contractor. No payment was missed or even late. When the building was dedicated, debt free, a wonderful sense of joy in what God had done pervaded the congregation.

When congratulations go to people, there is approval, admiration, and a sense of gratitude, which is certainly appropriate in itself. But when the glory focuses on what God has done, there is an outbreak of sheer joy, in which everyone shares.

It is important to note that this experience did not become a pattern or method for future undertakings in the congregation. We did not wait around for unexpected gifts of money before we started new projects. The lesson, rather, was a reminder that the Lord of this congregation had plans and resources beyond our knowing. No project should be undertaken without first hearing from Him.

This experience encouraged us to reckon on the active leadership of our divine Captains in a practical and realistic way.

Scripture links guidance to faith. The letter of James in the New Testament pinpoints an essential aspect of a prayer for guidance: "If any of you lacks wisdom, he should ask God, who gives generously to all without finding fault, and it will be given to him. But when he asks, *he must believe and not doubt*." The answer may not come at once, but from the moment the prayer leaves your lips, God expects you to believe that your prayer will be answered, "because he who doubts is like a wave of the sea, blown and tossed by the wind. That man should not think that he will receive anything from the Lord; he is a double-minded man, unstable in all he does" (James 1:5–8).

A prayer for guidance is not a shot in the dark: "Maybe He will answer, and then again, maybe He won't." God says, "If you lack wisdom, I will give it to you. *Ask* me. *Believe* me."

Bill Sy, a student in one of the seminaries of our church, once wrote and asked if he could do his internship in our congregation—a year of practical training and experience, one of the requirements in his seminary program. We read his letter and discussed it at a meeting of the church council.

An intern can augment the ministry of a congregation, even allowing for the fact that the pastor may have to commit time to the seminarian's instruction and training. At the time, however, we had a full staff; we did not see the need for an intern. Also, the responsibility for training an intern could encroach on my involvement in several new ministries that we had launched. There was not much enthusiasm for the idea. The time did not seem right.

After we had discussed it at some length, Bob Scott said, "Let's pray about it." As we prayed, a sense of release seemed to move among us. Tom Brown prayed, "Lord, we are not very interested in this thing, but you are at liberty to turn us around." And that is exactly what God did.

We had looked at the matter through the prism of common sense, which is one of the tools the Holy Spirit may use in guiding us. But times will come when the Holy Spirit sees that common sense is too shortsighted to see God's purpose. The thing that looks logical to us, for reasons we cannot see, does not fit in with God's plan.

Guidance does not necessarily come quickly. In our experience, it more often came over at least a short period of time. Yet at this meeting, God turned every one of us around right while we prayed. We came to the unanimous conviction that we should respond positively to this young man's letter and invite him to come to our congregation for his internship. When we began to pray, we did not realize that God would give us an answer right then and there. As a group, however, we were ready to lay down our preconceived notions. We were ready for God to act. We asked and believed.

A month or so later, Luthor Nelson, our youth worker, came in and told me he had decided to go to the seminary. We had talked about this possibility for some time; the decision had crystallized for him and his wife over the past several weeks.

This opened a slot in the staff of the congregation, ready-made for Bill Sy. He turned out to be a young man full of ideas and energy in his ministry with the youth, a gifted preacher and teacher. Years later, members still remembered his internship year with gratitude and affection.

Yet when the decision was made, none of this was known to us. The Holy Spirit led us simply to *ask* and *believe*.

Scripture links guidance to obedience. Obedience in your life journey expresses two things toward the One who leads you: *trust* and *love*. You obey because you trust the One who commands you. Like Moses, you commit yourself exclusively to His leadership: "The Lord alone led him; no foreign god was with him" (Deuteronomy 32:12). Your obedience, in turn, is the most unambiguous expression of love you can offer, as Jesus indicated when He said, "If you love me, you will obey what I command" (John 14:15).

In early June 1805, the Voyage of Discovery came to a fork in the Missouri River that presented a puzzling challenge. "An interesting question was now to be determined," Lewis wrote. "Which of these rivers was the Missouri?" He realized what a fateful decision they now faced. If they chose the wrong fork at this time of year, the delay would dishearten the party and might defeat the expedition altogether.

The captains and the Corps of Discovery came to a division of opinion. The north fork, Lewis wrote, ran "in the same boiling and roiling manner which has characterized the Missouri throughout its whole course so far." The entire party pronounced the north fork to be the true Missouri. Lewis noted pithily, "If myself and Captain Clark were to give our opinions, I believe we should be in the minority."

Lewis and Clark correctly discerned that the muddy water of the north fork indicated a long passage through open plain country. The clear water of the south fork suggested a river flowing more directly from the mountains, where the Mandan Indians had told them they would find the source of the Missouri.

When it came time to decide which fork the party would follow, the Corps of Discovery paid their finest tribute to the leadership of Lewis and Clark.

Lewis wrote: "All of the party except myself and Captain Clark were still firm in the belief that the north fork was the Missouri and that which we ought to take; *they said very cheerfully that they were ready to follow us any where we thought proper to direct, but they still thought that the other fork was the Missouri River."* They followed Lewis and Clark on the south fork, toward the mountains.

Had the Corps of Discovery taken the north fork, they would have lost precious time in a fruitless exploration of a tributary of the Missouri River. They would not have made it over the Rocky Mountains before winter set in. Whether they could have survived another winter and pressed on the following year is doubtful. The entire expedition could have failed.

When you Ride the River, divine guidance—obedience to the leadership of Jesus Christ and the Holy Spirit—is no optional luxury. It is an everyday necessity. It spells the difference between veering off course, going in circles—even sliding backwards!—or proceeding on toward the goal that God has set for your life journey.

The test of obedience comes at the point where the will of the soldier and the will of the commander cross. If we want to know the will of God, we must break off the love affair we have with our own will. The first step in finding and following God's plan is to lay your own plan on the table and say very cheerfully, "I am ready to follow you anywhere you think proper to direct!"

Gifts of the Holy Spirit

The Bible says the Holy Spirit may communicate with us through spiritual gifts, or *charisms*. The manifestation of spiritual gifts is often closely related to the inner witness of the Holy Spirit; inner witness may come, or be confirmed, through the manifestation of a gift of the Spirit, such as a "word of wisdom," "word of knowledge," "prophecy," or some other spiritual gift. The Holy Spirit may manifest a spiritual gift through you, or it may come to you through another person.

Guidance may come through a word of prophecy. One of the best examples of guidance in Scripture took place in the church at Antioch:

Now in the church at Antioch there were prophets and

teachers, Barnabas, Simeon who was called Niger, Lucius of Cyrene, Manaen a member of the court of Herod the tetrarch, and Saul. While they were worshiping the Lord and fasting, the Holy Spirit said, "Set apart for me Barnabas and Saul for the work to which I have called them." Then after fasting and praying they laid their hands on them and sent them off. (Acts 13:1–3 RSV)

How did they know that the Holy Spirit wanted them to set apart Barnabas and Saul? Did they hear a voice from heaven?

More likely, someone spoke a word of prophecy, for we are told "there were prophets and teachers." The assembly was gathered together, they were fasting and praying, they were seeking to respond to the initiatives of God. Someone in the assembly stood up and spoke something that he or she believed was from the Lord, a word of prophecy. The Holy Spirit brought God's NOW word into the assembly by means of a spiritual gift.

Notice, however, that the process of discernment does not end with a word from a prophet. The congregation continued to fast and pray. They *tested* the word. Prophetic words must be confirmed. "Two or three prophets should speak, and the others should weigh carefully what is said" (1 Corinthians 14:29).

One of the basic characteristics of a prophet is a willingness, indeed an eagerness, to have his words weighed in the body of believers. If someone claims to speak a prophetic word but resists correction, we should be cautious about accepting the word.

In Antioch, they weighed the words of the prophets. Only then did they conclude that a word was from the Lord. They prayed for Saul and Barnabas and sent them on their way.

You can well imagine that the prophetic word, confirmed by fellow believers, provided comfort for Saul (later called Paul) . . . when Elymas the sorcerer opposed him and tried to turn a Roman official against him (Acts 13:6–12) . . . and when opponents stoned him in the city of Lystra (Acts 14:19–20).

When you travel an uncertain or self-chosen path and problems rear up, fear and despair will come nipping at your heels; the path ahead will be dark. But when you Ride the River of *God's* empowering presence, difficulties evoke faith. You think of the Father who commissioned you; you look to your divine Captains who lead you. In times of difficulty, the Holy Spirit will often comfort or encourage us through one of the spiritual gifts. We need to cultivate an awareness and expectation of Him communicating in this way.

Spiritual gifts may confirm a NOW word of God. In our experience, gifts of the Holy Spirit confirm, more often than initiate, a work or plan of God. Scripture does not include all the details of that prayer meeting in Antioch, but I have a hunch Saul and Barnabas had been talking about going on a missionary journey for some time before the prophets spoke out. They had an urgency to spread the gospel. They had some acquaintance with the territory of Asia Minor. Yet they did not want to take off simply on the basis of their own reason or enthusiasm; they wanted to go out with a specific call from God, under the anointing of the Holy Spirit. The word of prophecy may well have come as a confirmation of something God had already kindled in their hearts.

We have seen this happen in many ordinary situations. People come for prayer. The person praying for them does not have specific knowledge about them or their situation. Yet as they pray, the Lord gives a word that confirms—or perhaps comments upon—something already at work in the person's thoughts and life.

Something similar could surface in a counseling session or in normal conversation. But when the word comes through a gift of the Holy Spirit, it can have a special impact. It catches one's attention because it comes by revelation rather than by human reason or counsel.

I think of a husband and wife who were facing some decisions about their family business. They came to a prayer service at our church one Sunday afternoon. The person who prayed for them said, "I have a sense that you are skating on thin ice in regard to some financial situation." The person praying had an inner image of someone skating on thin ice in regard to finances; he did not know anything about the decisions the family faced.

The husband and wife went home and checked over their records. They discovered two important items they had overlooked. They were able to make necessary adjustments. Their financial situation was already in their thinking. The Lord came quietly alongside and provided a helpful comment through a spiritual gift.

A word of wisdom or a word of knowledge may give us God's perspective, or comment, on some practical matter in our life.

When I was invited to do ministry outside our congregation, the men's prayer group would gather around, lay hands on me, and pray for the ministry I would be doing. Bob Scott, one of our elders, would often speak a word of knowledge—a prayer or comment on some aspect of the mission that was a private concern to me but about which he had no direct knowledge. He probably did not even realize he was doing this; he was simply in the Spirit, and the Spirit elected to manifest a spiritual gift through him.

After our congregation experienced a spiritual awakening, we discovered that gifts of the Holy Spirit are much more ordinary and closer at hand than we sometimes realize. You may be listening to a sermon, participating in a Bible study, or someone may come up and begin talking to you. Suddenly you realize that they are talking about something you have been thinking about privately all week long. You wonder, *How did they know I was thinking about that?*—and you may shrug it off as an interesting coincidence.

Most pastors have had the experience of someone coming out of a service, saying, "You were sure talking to me today!" What helped the person may not even have been in the sermon notes, just something thrown in. But the Lord knew the situation, and through the sermon brought a special word of revelation.

Spiritual gifts—words of prophecy and revelation—can pierce through walls of ignorance and misunderstanding to the heart of a matter. In counseling, for instance, through a spiritual gift, God can bring a NOW word that saves hours of beating around bushes.

John Bickersteth, an Anglican vicar in England, told me about an experience he had in counseling a disturbed young man whose life was a mess. "Nothing I said or did seemed to help. Then, one day, when I was taking a walk in the woods, the Lord spoke to me very clearly, 'The problem is his drinking. Tackle that, and the rest will follow.' " It was a new thought because the vicar did not know that the man had a drinking problem.

The next time he met with him, the young man mentioned casually, "I was down at the pub . . ."

The vicar said, "Let's stop there. Let's talk about your drinking."

The young man did not think his drinking was a problem, but as they talked further it was as if a knot began to unravel. The healing process began.

The Lord Communicates With Us Through Circumstances

The Lord Jesus and the Holy Spirit communicate with us in and through the circumstances of our everyday lives. Their communication through circumstances can be quite clear, but it is indirect. They speak to us through the words of other people. They help us read the meaning of unfolding events. They quietly direct our thoughts and prayers until we come to a place where we recognize their purpose. They underscore the requirements of our station or calling in life.

This indirect manner of "speaking" is appropriate to the way God relates to us during our life journey. When another human being steps into our field of awareness, we register his presence with our physical senses. We see him, hear him, touch him. We register the Lord's presence differently: not with our physical senses, but with faith. Occasionally the Lord may communicate with us by addressing our senses, but this is unusual. He reminds us in Scripture that, according to His plan, we "walk by faith, not by sight" (2 Corinthians 5:7 NKJV). The Lord Jesus and the Holy

Spirit "speak" to us in subtle and indirect ways because faith thrives best in the environment of things *hoped for*, things *not seen* (Hebrews 11:1). For reasons we may not fully understand, *faith* is particularly precious to God and necessary for us. It is His chosen way for us to maintain a living relationship with Him during our life journey. "Without faith it is impossible to please God" (Hebrews 11:6). When God reveals His will to us through the unfolding of a circumstance rather than booming His voice out of heaven, something is built into us, and into His Kingdom, that would otherwise be absent or lost.

The Lord May Speak to Us Through the Counsel of Other People

On some occasions Lewis and Clark involved the Corps of Discovery in making decisions. When courts-martial were convened to deal with serious discipline matters, nine of the men sat on the court. Clark attended to the form and rules without giving his opinion. After the judgment was rendered, the captains confirmed the sentence of the court.

In another matter, they decided where to build Fort Clatsop, their winter camp near the mouth of the Columbia River in 1805–06, by a vote in which all participated, including Clark's black servant, York, and the Indian woman, Sacagawea.

Counsel involves more than simply giving or receiving advice that is consistent with biblical principles. It is a dynamic undertaking in which Jesus Christ and the Holy Spirit are active, making known God's will in specific circumstances.

The counsel of fellow believers is one of the ways that God speaks to us in everyday life. In the Lutheran *Book of Concord*, the "mutual conversation and consolation of the brethren" is called a "means of grace"—one of the special ways that the grace of God comes to people.[3]

Good counsel serves to protect God's people. "Where there is no guidance, a people falls; but in an abundance of counselors there is safety" (Proverbs 11:14 RSV). Where mature Christian counsel is at hand and respected, people have a safe setting in which to share a word that they believe is from the Lord. If what they share is inaccurate or incomplete, others are standing by to help interpret or correct what they say. In this kind of setting, spiritual gifts of revelation can flower in a wholesome way.

I speak of *mature* Christian counsel to distinguish unseasoned spiritual discernment, or mere human opinion, from the judgment of those who have traveled some distance with the Lord—people steeped in the truth of Scripture, who have learned to recognize a NOW word of the Lord, and who know something of the situation under question.

The goal of counsel is to discern the mind of the Lord, not to win an argument or to find someone who agrees with you. Some people trek from counselor to counselor until they find someone who agrees with them, then confidently declare, "I have a word from the Lord." In the presence of counsel, one must hold one's own understanding, preference, or plan in an open hand.

The Old Testament records a conversation that took place between Jehoshaphat, the king of Judah, and Ahab, the king of Israel. They agreed to make war on the king of Ramoth Gilead, who had stolen land from Israel. They consulted with four hundred prophets, who prophesied a great victory. The king of Judah, however, felt uneasy about the counsel they were receiving.

"Jehoshaphat asked, 'Is there not a prophet of the Lord here whom we can inquire of?' The king of Israel answered Jehoshaphat, 'There is still one man through whom we can inquire of the Lord, but I hate him because he never prophesies anything good about me, but always bad. He is Micaiah son of Imlah.' "

When they called Micaiah in, he said, "The Lord has put a lying spirit in the mouths of all these prophets of yours. The Lord has decreed disaster for you" (1 Kings 22:7–8, 23). And so it happened: Ahab was killed in the battle; his army was routed.

The biblical idea of counsel cannot be equated with an agreeable idea or majority opinion, and certainly not with the latest poll! Biblical counsel is one of the ways by which God may speak to His people. The result of biblical counsel is that human opinion and desire bow to the will and purpose of God.

When this understanding takes root in a Christian home or congregation or community, counsel becomes more than an exchange of ideas or opinions. It is recognized as a means God may use to speak His NOW word into a specific situation.

Some years ago Jim Schmidt, an elder in our congregation, received a job offer that would take him out of our community. He and his family were deeply involved in the life of the congregation. Humanly speaking, he did not want to move away, nor did any of us want to see him go. Yet as we prayed about it, we came to a unanimous conviction that he should take the job. He moved away reluctantly, yet with a confidence that this was the way God was leading him.

Some years later we met and he shared what had happened in his life. "It was one of the toughest decisions I ever had to make," he said, "but time and again the Lord has confirmed that He was leading me by the hand."

The counsel of people from outside the community of believers is another way that God may bring a NOW word to His people.

At critical points in the Lewis and Clark expedition, help and counsel from outside the Corps of Discovery spelled the difference between defeat and victory. When they faced the Rocky Mountains, neither the written instructions of President Jefferson nor their own experience could direct them. On the westward crossing an old warrior of the Shoshone tribe guided them. On the eastward return two young men of the Nez Percé tribe expertly led them over a snow-covered trail.

In the Old Testament when the people of Israel had come out of Egypt and were encamped at Mount Sinai, Moses got bogged down with the responsibilities of leadership. His father-in-law,

Jethro, came to visit him. Jethro was not an Israelite. When he saw what Moses was doing, he gave him some advice on setting priorities and delegating responsibility. Moses recognized Jethro's counsel as a word from God. He "listened to his father-in-law and did everything he said" (Exodus 18:1–27).

Counsel often comes through ordered relationships. God may speak to us through a relationship that He has established. The apostle Paul underscores this in a remarkable passage where the authority in question is civil government. "Everyone must submit himself to the governing authorities, for there is no authority except that which God has established. . . . [The authority] is God's servant to do you good" (Romans 13:1–4). Paul wrote this when the pagan government of imperial Rome held sway. In these verses, the issue does not hinge on whether a government is good or just or mindful of God. The Apostle looks beyond any particular ruler to inspire faith in the overarching rule of God.

Family life is viewed in the same way, under the rule of God. "The head of every man is Christ, and the head of the woman is man, and the head of Christ is God" (1 Corinthians 11:3).

Order and authority in family relationships stem from the rule of God. The rule, however, is not simply imposed from the outside. The Lord himself is realistically, even if mysteriously, present and active in families. "Wives, submit to your husbands as to the Lord. For the husband is head of the wife as Christ is the head of the church. . . . Husbands, love your wives, just as Christ loved the church and gave himself up for her. . . . This is a profound mystery—but I am talking about Christ and the church. . . . Children, obey your parents in the Lord. . . . Fathers, do not exasperate your children; instead, bring them up in the training and instruction of the Lord" (Ephesians 5:22–6:4).

In their relationships with one another, family members express the image of God on earth; they identify with God and with His purpose. The headship of a husband is modeled on the self-giving love of Christ. The submission of wife and children models

147

the bridal love of the church for Christ.

The idea of a person in authority lording it over those under his authority is alien to the thought world of the Bible. Jesus said, "The rulers of the Gentiles lord it over them, and their high officials exercise authority over them. Not so with you. Instead, whoever wants to become great among you must be your servant . . . just as [I] did not come to be served, but to serve, and to give [my] life as a ransom for many" (Matthew 20:25–28).

In the setting of a family, the purpose of counsel comes to light in the clearest way: it is a means by which God involves himself in the lives of people to show them His will and purpose.

From what I have observed in marriages under my pastoral care and in my own marriage, a husband and wife committed to knowing and following God's will come to most of their decisions by common agreement, which is not surprising, since they are tuned in to the same source.

The Bible also uses the language of family to describe a congregation of Christians. The church is called "God's *household*" (1 Timothy 3:15). Believers relate to one another as fathers, brothers, mothers, sisters (1 Timothy 5:1–2). The rule of God is mediated through family-like relationships. The apostle Paul counsels believers in Galatia as a parent speaking to a child (Galatians 4:19).

The practice of having a spiritual director, or mentor, has a long history in the Catholic tradition; it has found fresh acceptance in some renewal groups looking for better ways to encourage spiritual growth and development in our individualistic Western culture. Some men's groups, for example, encourage one-on-one relationships; a spiritual novice voluntarily seeks to be mentored by a man of greater maturity. Positive testimonies from these relationships abound. Time and again you hear it said that the counsel one receives outstrips the knowledge or wisdom of the mentor himself; he is a channel through which God speaks His mind and will into a man's life.

Godly counsel is more than good human advice. It is a means God may use to speak His will into particular situations.

Counsel may confirm God's will by bringing people to unity. When God has a NOW word for an individual or group, one of the ways He may confirm it is by bringing a group of believers to one mind. The experience goes by different names. Quakers call it the "sense of the meeting." Some communities speak of "unanimity." Others describe it as "group guidance." Whatever term you use, it is a recognition that Jesus Christ and the Holy Spirit exercise active leadership when Christians counsel together. They can bring a group of believers to a common conviction concerning God's will, a conviction in which everyone shares.

Unity wrought by the Holy Spirit may be straightforward agreement about a particular matter. It can, however, be more subtle and complex. The Spirit may lead a person to yield wholeheartedly to the judgment of a brother or sister with whom he disagrees—without resolving the disagreement.

I remember when Roy Jones would take his turn at ushering in our church. He walked with a cane in each hand because he had multiple sclerosis and was beginning to experience some of its crippling effects. He told me that he found the idea of spiritual healing, or healing through prayer, hard to believe. He was an engineer who described himself as "a practical man." Nevertheless, during a men's retreat he agreed to be prayed for, and he was wonderfully healed. The healing was confirmed in all his medical records. His understanding of what was practical expanded to include healing through prayer. In the years that followed he prayed for the sick in our congregation and at the local hospital as a lay chaplain.

He once shared with me a curious sidelight to his experience. "The Lord has given me faith for healing," he said. "But when it comes to finances, the old engineer mentality kicks back into gear. If an issue of finances comes up in the church council, I have to back off and let Bud Hahn take the lead; he has faith for finances."

Roy saw that unity is rooted in something deeper than mere natural agreement. In a given situation, the Spirit may achieve unity by giving special authority to the word of a person through whom He chooses to speak in that situation.

In a family, Spirit-wrought unity between husband and wife strengthens confidence in God's will and plan for the family. It also fosters a spirit of peace in the family. When the will of God prevails, the contest of human wills is laid aside. There may be differences, even spirited argument, but aimed at discerning God's will, not at winning an argument or getting my own way.

Jim Canfield, a friend of ours, once said to his wife, Sharon, "I will entertain anything you say to me as though it were my own thought." That shows understanding; a wise husband knows that God may often speak to him, and to the family, through the thoughts and words of his wife. The same is true for the wife as she considers the words of her husband. Disagreements do not set husband and wife against one another but more earnestly *with* one another. To discover God's will in and through a time of disagreement is a daunting—but rewarding!—undertaking.

When you Ride the River, following the leadership of Jesus Christ and the Holy Spirit is the primary requirement. Day by day it is the starting point for "proceeding on" in the journey God has set before you. When you push out into the river, it can be a tremendous encouragement to faith if the Lord has confirmed His will by bringing about a Spirit-wrought unity with other believers.

The Lord May Speak to Us Through the Unfolding of Events

A major strand in the prophetic tradition of the Old Testament was an inspired interpretation of actual events. Isaiah saw the Persian king Cyrus fulfilling God's purpose, though Cyrus did not acknowledge God (Isaiah 45:1–7). During a troubled time in Judah, Jeremiah's cousin came to him, offering to sell him a field that would become valuable at a later time. Jeremiah wrote, "I knew that this was the word of the Lord; so I bought the field" (Jeremiah 32:8–9).

The meaning of an event may not come to light at once. We must allow time for the Holy Spirit to help us read His meaning in a particular event.

Our congregation once gave me a sabbatical leave to do some research and writing. We needed to find someone who could take my place in the congregation for a year. We drew up a list of about a dozen people. I thought the list included several excellent possibilities, but all the people we called said they were not available.

After about ten calls I began to think, *Lord, are you telling me that you don't want me to go? Nobody seems to be available.* Then Harold Eimon, a missionary in Japan, came to mind. I called him and he said yes, they were coming home on furlough. He didn't want to do a lot of traveling. They wanted to spend most of the year in one place, where their children could be settled in school. Our parsonage, of course, would be available and was quite adequate for their large family. The arrangement worked out well. The Eimons spent the year in San Pedro and maintained a relationship with the congregation for many years following.

As I look back on it, I see that the Lord wanted me to persevere in the plan for a sabbatical. He was testing and stretching our faith in regard to something that He was calling us to do. God does indeed speak through circumstances, but we need to be on guard against reading circumstances too quickly or superficially. We need the guidance of the Holy Spirit to read accurately what He is saying to us in a particular set of circumstances.

Events alter strategy, not purpose. Lewis and Clark demonstrated in extraordinary degree the twin requisites of successful military commanders—resoluteness and flexibility.[4] They were guided by the commission of President Jefferson from the day they headed upstream from St. Louis. Yet when circumstances clearly required a change of strategy or an unanticipated decision, they made the necessary adjustment.

Before leaving the Mandan country in North Dakota they sent a boat with some men and a full report back to St. Louis, according to their agreement with President Jefferson. They intended to send a second report back to St. Louis when they reached the Great Falls of the Missouri. When they got there, however, they had not yet made contact with the Shoshone Indians and did not know whether they would be friendly or hostile. The captains decided they needed all their men and could not afford to dispatch a canoe back to St. Louis. When a report did not arrive in St. Louis, many people concluded that the whole expedition had perished. The captains' decision showed both the *seriousness* of adapting strategy to particular circumstances and also its sometime *necessity*.

Events, in themselves, may be ambiguous. The Holy Spirit must help us read them accurately.

On his third missionary journey through Asia Minor, the apostle Paul came to the Jewish synagogue in Ephesus. He "spoke boldly there for three months, arguing persuasively about the kingdom of God. But some of them became obstinate; they refused to believe and publicly maligned the Way. So Paul left them. He took the disciples with him and had discussions daily in the lecture hall of Tyrannus" (Acts 19:8–9). Paul sensed in this situation, where people were stiffening their necks against the gospel, that God was closing a door, telling him to move out and hold meetings somewhere else.

Jesus, however, told a parable in which a closed door had the opposite meaning. A man knocks on his friend's door at midnight; despite rebuffs, he continues to knock until the friend finally comes to the door (Luke 11:5–8). He does not let discouraging circumstances deter him.

In Ephesus, a closed door called for a change in strategy. In the parable, a closed door called for perseverance in faith and prayer. In both situations, God speaks through the circumstance of a closed door, but the Holy Spirit must clarify the meaning. We need the guidance of the Spirit to read accurately what God may be saying to us in particular situations.

Events may set aside our well laid plans precisely in order to advance us toward the goal. One of Lewis's pet projects was a light boat frame that he invented for use in the upper reaches of the Missouri River, where the Corps would not be able to portage large rivercraft. It was brilliant in conception, but when the time came to use it, they could not find enough pitch or gum to make it watertight. Lewis wrote that he had to give up "all further hope of using my favorite boat." His priority was clear: they buried the boat and proceeded on.

Times of divine silence can be important events in our life journey. Lutheran pastor Klaus Hess had a favorite saying: "There are three keys to discovering God's will for your life: patience, patience, and patience." This is particularly apt when God seems to be saying nothing at all. Answers to prayers for His direction do not necessarily drop into place the same moment, or day, or week that we pray. God guides us in His own way, according to His own timetable. Also, He may guide us in ways, and at times, when we are unaware of it. He doesn't necessarily alert us to everything He is doing in connection with our life journey. We have no way of knowing how many other things may be linked together with our prayers in His master plan. Living quietly and confidently with the silences of God is a normal experience as you Ride the River.

On occasion we may lay out a fleece to confirm what God is saying to us. The term comes from the story of Gideon, in the Old Testament.

> Gideon said to God, "If you will save Israel by my hand as you have promised—look, I will place a wool fleece on the threshing floor. If there is dew only on the fleece and all the ground is dry, then I will know that you will save Israel by my hand, as you said." And that is what happened. Gideon rose early the next day; he squeezed the fleece and wrung out the dew—a bowlful of water. Then Gideon said to God, "Do not be angry with me. Let me make just one more request. Allow

me one more test with the fleece. This time make the fleece dry and the ground covered with dew." That night God did so. Only the fleece was dry; all the ground was covered with dew. (Judges 6:36–40)

The value of a "fleece" is that it is something over which we have no direct influence or control. It is objective. It can be particularly helpful when we recognize the need to discriminate between our own feelings about something—strong desire, fear, personal concern—and God's will in the matter.

It is not something one does casually or frequently. It is somewhat like drawing straws (Acts 1:26 TLB) or choosing a Scripture at random. Accompanying it must be the conviction that God gives you the freedom to do it in a particular situation.

At one point, the youth program in our congregation started expanding faster than we could keep up with it. It looked as if we needed a second pastor or a full-time youth worker. Yet we wanted to test the idea, in case it would prove to be just our own good idea rather than God's will.

We prayed about it in the church council. Keith Goble said, "Let's lay out a fleece. If a certain amount of money comes in over the next three months—above what we normally receive—we will take that as the Lord's indication that we should call a second pastor or a youth worker." We talked and prayed further. The idea commended itself to everyone on the council.

Week by week we watched the offerings come in. They began to inch up. We got excited. "The Lord is answering our prayer. The fleece is getting wet!" On the final Sunday of the test period, we were hanging over the shoulders of the money counters as they totaled the day's offering.

We came up fifty dollars short of the goal. One of the men reached in his pocket and said, "I'll give another fifty dollars!" But the others intervened, "Oh no you won't! That's exactly what we don't want. If we try to manipulate things, we will be stuck with our own project."

We recognized that the Lord had said no, but in a gentle way, almost like, "Not quite. Not yet."

Lou Hefner, a layman in the congregation, stepped into the breach and took over the youth program. Two years later, leading in a quite different way, the Lord brought Paul Anderson to the congregation, a second pastor who would remain more than twenty years. To begin with he worked with the youth, then branched into other areas of ministry as well. We served together for eleven years. When I left to take another call, Paul became the senior pastor.

Looking back on it, we could see that God's plans went beyond the immediate pressure of a burgeoning youth program. As we responded in a realistic way to His guidance, He could lead us into His plan step by step.

The first step in an undertaking is often important. The Lord may give you something to encourage you at the outset, a kind of snapshot of its spiritual direction and significance. Any step that you take forward, following Jesus Christ and the Holy Spirit, will sooner or later evoke a counterreaction from the devil. God knows that you may need the memory of something encouraging to fall back on when you come up against hardship and opposition. Therefore, He often gives something vividly encouraging early on as an antidote to the discouragement you may face later.

We once initiated an intensive Bible study program for the youth of our church, beginning with fourth graders. The program exploded in our small congregation. Fourth, fifth, and sixth graders met for a fellowship supper every Wednesday evening, followed by Bible study in small groups. There was a liveliness and joy among these young people that was infectious.

Our objective was to give the children an overview of the entire Bible over a three-year period. Because there was no material available with this kind of aim, I had to write it. I found myself scribbling out the lessons week by week, mimeographing them, trying gamely to stay one lesson ahead of the children. Each of the small Bible study groups was led by an adult. We had a level of involvement by laypeople that we had never before experienced. We were running ourselves ragged trying to keep up with what was happening with these kids. Yet the Lord gave us such first-step encouragement that we never seriously doubted we were on the track of His will and purpose.

It took seven years to get the program fully developed and functioning in the congregation.[5] We faced mountains of work and substantial difficulties. Sandra Hall, our education director, wrote a teacher's guide for every lesson. Some parents thought the program was too demanding of the children—until their own children completed it, then they became outspoken advocates! At the beginning, the Lord gave us an encouraging glimpse of the effect that serious Bible study could have with young children. His encouragement at the beginning kept us going when things got tough.

The Lord Speaks to Us Through Our Calling or Station in Life

On August 22, 1804, Lewis and Clark ordered a vote for a sergeant to replace Charles Floyd, who had died two days earlier (the only death that the Corps of Discovery would experience throughout the expedition). Patrick Gass received nineteen votes. He at once fell heir to the catalog of responsibilities and privileges that went with the rank. The outcome of his promotion was so ordinary and predictable that it scarcely merited mention; Lewis noted tersely in the Orderly Book that Gass would immediately assume the prescribed duties of a sergeant.

Many everyday decisions follow simply and naturally from a particular station or calling that we occupy in life: we are husbands, wives, children; employers, employees; citizens, students, soldiers, members of voluntary organizations. The decision of a mother to feed and dress her child, the decision of a citizen to pay his taxes, the decision of a student to get up and go to school scarcely qualify as choices. They are, in a sense, predetermined by one's position or responsibilities.

Yet in a culture in which individual choice routinely overrules every other consideration, it is well to underscore the moral symmetry of the Bible: particular callings, or stations in life, involve particular responsibilities.

> Each one of you [husbands] must love his wife as he loves himself, and the wife must respect her husband. (Ephesians 5:33)
> Jesus said, "If anyone would come after me, he must deny himself and take up his cross and follow me" (Matthew 16:24).
> Everyone must submit himself to the governing authorities, for there is no authority except that which God has established. (Romans 13:1)

Many more Bible verses like these could be cited. According to one's station in life—if, say, one is a husband, a wife, a disciple, a citizen—the Bible has a standard against which choices and decisions must be measured.

A citizen may need special guidance on HOW to show respect for governing authority. The decision to do so, however, has already been made; it belongs to the calling of a Christian citizen.

A believer may sense the Holy Spirit putting His finger on something and saying, "This must be dealt with" or "This must be given up." Specific issues will differ from one believer to another. Yet the basic direction for every follower of Jesus is settled at the outset: Say NO to your own will and say YES to Jesus.

The way that the Lord Jesus Christ and the Holy Spirit lead us in everyday life will respect—will take into account—the responsibilities that pertain to a calling or a position in life. This does not mean that divine guidance will proceed along rigid, legalistic lines. Indeed, the Lord may lead us through times when the usual way of living out our calling does not match up with the will of God. The apostles in Jerusalem lived under, and respected, the authority of the religious leaders who ruled the Jewish community. Yet when the authorities ordered the apostles to cease teaching about Jesus, they replied, "We must obey God rather than men!" (Acts 5:29).

That having been said, the truth remains that our divine Captains lead us to fulfill faithfully the particular callings we have in life.

The Lord Speaks to Us Through Sanctified Common Sense

"Use your common sense!" is a shorthand way of saying, "Think reasonably. Be logical, practical." When you become a Christian, concerned about following Jesus Christ and the Holy Spirit, you do not deposit your brains at the door of the church and suddenly become "spiritual." God expects us to use the minds He has given us.

But a new dimension is added. The Bible says, "Do not conform any longer to the pattern of this world, but be transformed by the *renewing of your mind*" (Romans 12:2).

A renewed mind operates with more than common sense. It uses *sanctified* common sense. Sanctified common sense looks at a situation and says, "How will this situation be affected if, or as, God intervenes?" The reasoning process is not complete until the possibility of the Holy Spirit's intervention has been factored into an equation.

An illustration from Scripture comes to mind, the incident in which Peter walks on water (Matthew 14:28–30). If you were to lay it out like a mathematical formula, it would look something like this:

(one man, 165 pounds) + (long robe and sandals) + (high wind and waves) + (deep water) − (boat) = Sink

That is how the equation plays out, using common sense.

Now look at that same situation with *sanctified* common sense.

You still have the same elements, but you add another factor—the intervention of God:

(one man, 165 pounds) + (long robe and sandals) + (high wind and waves) + (deep water) − (boat) + (*the word of Christ, "Come!"*) = Walk!

Peter did not act illogically. He did not remove any factors from consideration. He simply added the word of Christ to the equation, and that changed the outcome.

Unusual interventions of God capture our attention—healings, miracles, visions, revelations. But God intervenes in our lives in many different ways. It may be quite ordinary, as simple as the quiet assurance of the Spirit that everything is okay: "Go ahead with what you are doing."

The early church lived with a constant sense of God's empowering presence. The manner of His intervention often surprised them, for it did not follow set patterns. The reality of His intervention, however, did not surprise them; they depended on it.

They experienced His intervention in many situations—in the midst of spirited debate; while they were gathered for prayer; when members came under rebuke; when new believers received the Holy Spirit; when they were threatened with shipwreck on a storm-tossed sea;[6] and, undoubtedly, they experienced, as we do, many quiet days unmarked by any unusual intervention of God.

Sanctified common sense reckons realistically on God's intervention, but the manner of His intervention is like an x-factor in an equation; to begin with, it is an unknown quantity. The Spirit must school us and lead us to perceive how God may intervene in each concrete situation.

"Green Light Guidance"

Someone might say, "Well, then, how *can* I be certain about divine guidance? It's nice to hear stories about people who get words or visions or read about such things in the Bible. But I never get anything like that. I struggle with a decision right up to the last moment, and even then I'm not one hundred percent sure that it's in line with God's will."

Actually, this probably describes how many people experience the leading of the Holy Spirit. For most people, most of the time, divine guidance is not a blazing certainty. You may describe it that way in hindsight; when you look backward, you can often see clearly how the Lord guided you. But in the moment of decision, it may be just a slight tilting in one direction, so slight that you wonder whether you dare act on it.

When it comes time to make a decision, many of us will find ourselves praying like this: "Lord, I have prayed about this. I have sought counsel. I have considered the circumstances. As best I understand it, you are telling me to make *this* decision. I sense a slight tilting in that direction. If I am wrong, Lord, roadblock me. But if I am hearing you correctly, give me green lights."

Recognizing a roadblock can be guidance that is as certain, and as necessary, as receiving a green light. A country western song lyric puts it succinctly: "Some of God's greatest gifts are unanswered prayers!"

"Green light guidance" means that you take tentative steps to begin with, steps that you can reverse if necessary. It is no less real guidance, but it is guidance that requires continual dependence on God.

The year I graduated from seminary, I was working as a copywriter at Augsburg Publishing House in Minneapolis. One afternoon my ballpoint pen ran out of ink. I walked to a nearby stationery store to get a refill. There I ran into Loren Halvorsen, a man I had known in college.

"I just got back from Germany," he told me. "I was driving through town and saw this store. Reminded me I needed some things."

So our paths crossed coincidentally, it would seem. In half an hour he would have been out of town, and I would not have seen him at all.

He told me a little bit about what he had done in Germany during a year of graduate study. Then he said, "By the way, some of the youth groups in Germany are doing interesting things in religious drama—evangelistic plays and so on. You were into that kind of thing back in college. Why don't you go over and study what they're doing? Maybe we could use it in the church here in America."

"Well, I don't know. I'm ready to graduate from the seminary. . ." I wasn't particularly interested. But as I went back to my office, the idea began to play around in my mind. Maybe it would be good to go to Germany, experience another culture. In the days following I made some inquiries. I applied for some scholarships and received enough financial help to get the family about halfway across the Atlantic Ocean.

It was not a strong impulse, just a slight tilting. I called Dr. Fred Schiotz, the president of our denomination. I told him I had received an inquiry from a congregation in California that was interested in calling a pastor from our graduating class, but I was thinking about going to Germany for a year before accepting a call.

He said, "Of course, calls to congregations come in all the time. This thing in Germany could be a special opportunity. Maybe you ought to do it." Not a commanding word, just a slight nudge.

Things worked out. My wife and I and our three small children went to Germany. Among other things, we learned to speak the German language. Only as we looked back on it, some years later, did we realize how significant this was in God's plan for us. Our congregation came to have close relationships with groups in Germany, groups that had much to teach us about spiritual renewal. Many of these contacts depended upon our being able to communicate with them in German. It was part of God's plan.

When I ran into a college classmate in that stationery store . . . when I spoke to the president of our denomination . . . God was giving our family a NOW word. No bolt from heaven; seemingly, we could easily have missed it. God gave us encouragement to take a step of faith. A slight tilting, a nudge. It was enough.

Don't be discouraged and say, "*I* never get a NOW word." If the Lord gives you a nudge, accept it. Step out in faith, ready for the Lord's plan to work out in your life—ready, also, to receive correction should it be needed. Living under the leadership of Jesus Christ and the Holy Spirit is something like learning to play the piano: lesson by lesson you learn to translate that formidable array of black notes into a beautiful flow of music. Along the way you strike some wrong notes, but no matter, that is the experience of every person who becomes a piano player.

The Obedience of Faith

When a NOW word is confirmed and the inner witness of the Holy Spirit increases in strength we come to the place where we must venture a step of obedience, what the apostle Paul calls *the obedience of faith* (Romans 1:5; 16:26). The obedience of faith is not reserved alone for the great issues surrounding our salvation; it is an everyday response to the leadership of our divine Captains. It is neither pious guesswork nor a mere I-hope-so approximation of God's will. It is grounded in spiritual discernment, a bold *Yes!* to the leadership of Jesus Christ and the Holy Spirit. Yet it proceeds in godly humility, saying, "If I have heard God inaccurately, or only in part, I trust that He will correct me and further reveal His will."

The obedience of faith inspires courage as we Ride the River. "I am where I am—I am doing what I am doing—because the Lord Jesus Christ and the Holy Spirit have so led me. Under their leadership, I am Riding the River. They will not leave me stranded halfway up the river."

To refuse to follow our divine Captains is not only disobedient, it is fundamentally foolish. Apart from their leadership we will never reach the goal the Father has set for us.

There is no greater joy than knowing that, however difficult it might be at the moment, what I am doing is the will of God. Real joy comes not simply from nice things that happen to us. People surrounded by luxury can be utterly miserable. That which puts an inextinguishable candle of joy in the depth of your life is the quiet persuasion, "I am living in the will of God; His empowering presence is with me."

The NOW Word of the Lord

The problem is not that God never speaks a NOW word. The problem is that we are too little experienced in hearing God speak to us personally—through Scripture, wise counsel, meaningful circumstances, thoughtful reflection, or gifts of the Holy Spirit. And we are too untried in faith to step out in obedience.

If I sense that God is speaking in one of these ways, it is a signal, first of all, to be alert. God will usually confirm a NOW word in more than one way. If, for instance, I see some circumstances through which God may be speaking—circumstances, but nothing more—I may be cautious. Or, I may have learned by experience that when I come up with a good idea, there is no automatic guarantee that it is *God's* idea. So I look for God to speak further, confirming a NOW word in ways of His own choosing.

The life of faith moves ever into the unknown, and often into warfare. When difficulty, or the battle, waxes hard, we have to know that God has put us where we are, and that our Captains are with us at every bend in the river.

When you Ride the River, you are moving:

- from a known point of beginning: *your new life in Christ*
- to a known destination: *eternal life in the kingdom of God*
- by a precise way: *the will of God*
- as yet unexplored: *dependent on the NOW word of God, the day-by-day leadership of the Lord Jesus Christ and the Holy Spirit.*

Ride the River evokes an image of action, challenge, hard work. It can be all of that and more. Yet paradoxically, discerning what Jesus Christ and the Holy Spirit are saying goes hand in hand with great patience, quiet, and waiting on the Lord: "Those who wait on the Lord Shall renew their strength; They shall mount up with wings like eagles, They shall run and not be weary, They shall walk and not faint" (Isaiah 40:31 NKJV).

CHAPTER SEVEN
RIDE THE RIVER!

*How do we Ride the River of God's empowering presence? We
remind ourselves again and again that the Lord Jesus Christ and the
Holy Spirit are with us to lead us on our journey.*

FOR MEMBERS OF the Corps of Discovery, the presence and authority of Lewis and Clark was close, always at hand. Charbonneau
once became exasperated with Sacagawea and struck her, which
he apparently considered his natural right as her husband. Clark
intervened and spoke sharply to him; there would be none of that.
When necessary, Clark's authority could be awesome.

Once, while reconnoitering on a high bluff above the Missouri
River, Lewis and Richard Windsor came on a stretch of greasy
mud. Lewis wrote in his journal that Windsor slipped over the
edge of the bluff and cried out, " 'God, God, Captain, what shall
I do. . . .' On turning about I found Windsor had slipped and
fallen, was lying prostrate on his belly, with his right hand, arm,
and leg over the precipice while he was holding on with the left
arm and foot as well as he could which appeared to be with much
difficulty. . . . I told him to take the knife out of his belt behind
him with his right hand and dig a hole with it in the face of the
bank to receive his right foot, which he did, and then raised himself to his knees. I then directed him to take off his moccasins and
to come forward on his hands and knees, holding the knife in one
hand and the gun in the other. This he happily effected and escaped." Whatever the circumstance, the captains acted decisively
in seeing to the care and protection of their party.

Some days of course were ordinary, predictable. The winter of 1805–06 at Fort Clatsop on the Pacific Coast had many such days. "Not any occurrences today worthy of notice" appears repeatedly in the log of that damp and dreary winter. Yet even during these monotonous months, the unexpected or dangerous could suddenly loom up. Clark wrote in his journal that they had to act swiftly to save one of the privates, Hugh McNeal, who narrowly escaped the plan of a pretended Indian friend to kill him for his blanket.

In every circumstance of life we need to remind ourselves that our divine Captains are present. They oversee every aspect of our life journey with love, authority, and care. The Father's plan for us depends on the wisdom and power of their leadership.

I was fresh out of seminary when I first experienced the gift of speaking in tongues. I had a head full of theology, but no experience with this kind of charismatic happening. I was ignorant both of the value of the gift and of problems it could provoke in our congregation.

The Lord graciously intervened in the person of David du Plessis, a Pentecostal preacher widely acquainted in Protestant and Catholic circles. He spoke at a meeting in our community, and afterward we talked together. He gave me wise, fatherly counsel: "Tell your wife and your bishop about your experience. Then be quiet for a time. Let God bring to you people who are ready to hear your testimony. If your people fail to see in you the marks of love and humility, they will have every reason to doubt the authenticity of your experience." A quiet word of wisdom.

Around the same time the Lord provided a contact with Klaus Hess and other Lutheran pastors in Germany. Some years earlier in their prayer fellowships they had experienced charismatic gifts, at that time still largely outside the experience of the Lutheran church. They shared with us counsel of wisdom and maturity that helped us greatly in the uncharted way that lay ahead. In speaking about the need to discern the difference between the leading of

God and our own thoughts and desires, Hess said, "When we are first awakened, we have almost no idea how deep the flesh goes. Divine guidance means divine refinement." Words of wisdom. The Lord's active leadership on a critical stretch of the River.

Following Jesus Christ and the Holy Spirit day by day does not mean a continual flow of surprising revelations. The settled experience is more a sense of the presence and watchful care of the triune God. Out of that assurance come specific words and acts of guidance that help you follow God's plan.

Leadership: Not by Principle, but by a Person

The leadership of Jesus Christ and the Holy Spirit is not a roundabout way of saying that we strive to live according to biblical principles. It is what the plain sense of the words mean: our divine Captains, as living persons, do actually lead us in everyday life; they are present with us; they guide us in the decisions that we face; they equip and empower us in the things that God calls us to do. That is the plan God the Father set out from the beginning.

It is not enough simply to believe in the truth and authority of God's Word and apply it as best we can, the way we might believe in the truth of a mathematical formula and put it to use. We can operate a mathematical formula at will and get a predictable result. God's Word is different. It is a *living* word, not an abstract principle.

Andrew Murray notes the difference between taking God at his word and taking the Word as God's:

> Men deal with the Word more than with the Living God. Faith has very truly been defined as "Taking God at His word." To many this means, "Taking the word as God's"; they didn't see the force of the thought, "*Taking God* at His word." A key or a door handle has no value until I use it for the lock and the door I want to open; it is alone in direct and living contact with God Himself that the Word will open the heart

to believe. The faith that enters into the inheritance is the attitude of soul which waits for *God Himself*.[1]

If we presume to understand or apply Scripture with human intellect alone, Scripture itself can become the instrument for missing or avoiding God's will. Man's first sin stemmed from a desire to live by independent human knowledge rather than out of a relationship with God. God told Adam and Eve not to eat of the Tree of the Knowledge of Good and Evil (see Genesis 2:17). He did not want them to base their life on a theoretical knowledge of good and evil, independent of their relationship with Him. Relationship with the triune God, not mastery of abstract principles, is the basis for proceeding on in our journey.

Guidance Is Grounded in the Call of Jesus

The foregoing chapters have underscored the reality of divine guidance. How God speaks to us and how we listen to Him have been described in some detail. It is good to emphasize, however, that these are only the most visible aspects of divine guidance. Underneath is the great root structure of a life that has heard and responded to the call of Jesus: "If anyone would come after me, he must deny himself and take up his cross and follow me. For whoever wants to save his life will lose it, but whoever loses his life for me will find it" (Matthew 16:24–25).

Becoming a follower of Jesus Christ is like leaving an old way of life on the dockside in St. Louis. You give your life over to the Captains. What they count important now becomes imperative to you.

Lewis and Clark expected men to set aside old habits when they joined the Corps of Discovery. In the spring of 1805, they added Sacagawea to the Corps of Discovery—a young wife with a new baby. She journeyed with the men from the Mandan villages of North Dakota to the Pacific Ocean and back. Stephen Ambrose paints a vivid picture of the softening influence of her womanly presence. Night by night around the campfire, sitting by her husband or nursing her baby, she was a token of home and family. For fifteen months she lived and ate and worked and camped in the midst of twenty-seven virile young men. No hint of an incident ever arose between her and any of the men in the Corps of Discovery. The captains would not have allowed it.[2]

Living with the Captains—the Lord Jesus and the Holy Spirit—has its effect on everything you do from morning till night. How you speak. How you get on with other members in the fellowship of believers. How you take up everyday tasks. How attentive you are to instruction. How faithfully you follow where the Captains want to lead you.

When you Ride the River, you slough off old ways. You take on a way of living that lines up with what the Captains expect. They shape your life to their demanding standards. Otherwise you develop no ear to listen, no will to follow where they want to lead you in order to accomplish God's plan.

Beyond Discipline to Discipleship

What distinguishes a well-disciplined life from the life of a disciple?

Discipline is something set before me, or laid on me. It may come from a book, from tradition, from someone in authority, or from the example of another person. Good discipline can have a wholesome effect on my life. By itself, however, it is a lonely undertaking.

Discipleship points beyond discipline to a *relationship*. There is one who teaches, one who learns; one in a position of authority, one in submission to authority; one who leads, one who follows.

When you Ride the River, your primary focus is on discipleship. Spiritual disciplines have a place, even an important place, but they grow out of your relationship with the triune God, who has taken up dwelling in your body. "Do you not know that your body is a temple of the Holy Spirit, who is in you, whom you have received from God?" (1 Corinthians 6:19). "I pray that out of [God's] glorious riches he may strengthen you with power through his Spirit in your inner being, so that Christ may dwell in your hearts through faith. And . . . that you may be filled to the measure of all the fullness of God" (Ephesians 3:16–19).

The presence, authority, and leadership of the triune God is the yardstick of reality for our journey. It is the ground of life and the portal of wisdom.

Nurturing the Indwelling Presence of God By Continual Acts of Remembrance

How does the Lord's presence become real when you Ride the River? The gateway to a vital relationship with God is what the Bible calls a renewed mind: "Do not conform any longer to the pattern of this world, but be transformed by the *renewing of your mind*. Then you will be able to test and approve what God's will is—his good, pleasing and perfect will" (Romans 12:2). Here we wish to focus on a single characteristic of a renewed mind:

> A renewed mind *continually reminds itself*, and rests in the assurance that God lives in me and I in Him.

Every morning when you wake up, and many times during the day, you step into conscious relationship with God by acts of faith. You *recurringly remind yourself* that the triune God lives in you and is in charge of your life journey.

God has clearly revealed that the life of a believer will be indwelt by His own life. On your lifelong voyage of discovery, the leadership of Jesus Christ and the Holy Spirit takes on shape and reality through recurring acts of faith. You "take every thought *captive* to obey Christ" (2 Corinthians 10:5 RSV). You are more than a person following a code of discipline. You are a living disciple of a living Lord. During times of great activity, or during times of quiet waiting, *you again and again remind yourself that your life is indwelt by the life and presence of the triune God.*

Crossover from Possibility to Reality

The subject of God's indwelling presence in the life of a believer is vast. Here I underscore a single aspect of it: *by continually reminding ourselves that the triune God is alive and present within us, we give place to His will for our lives.*

The world around us trumpets a thousand reminders every day, urging us to follow its ways. We need counter-reminders, telling us that the purpose and direction for our lives is not found in the world's quack prescriptions; it is in the hands of the God who indwells us. In each act of remembrance we *give up* our own will and way and *give over* to the living leadership of our divine Captains.

In a word, we align ourselves with truth. By acts of continual remembrance, the possibility that Jesus Christ and the Holy Spirit will lead us crosses over and becomes reality.

The Spirit may give us various words or concepts or images to remind ourselves afresh that God is in us and in charge. The experience will not follow a set pattern, lest we would begin to put confidence in a mental habit or formula.

The Spirit may enliven a single word of Scripture. For a time, it seems, that word springs up every time you turn around, reminding you that God is present and active.

I once experienced this when I heard a teaching by Bishop Don Meares on the word *grace*.[3] *Grace* is often defined as "unmerited favor." In his six-part study, Meares shows that this definition is not altogether adequate. "Unmerited favor," he suggests, is closer to the biblical meaning of *mercy*. In the thought-world of the early church, *grace* has a more dynamic meaning. Meares' definition captures the vitality and movement of the word, as it is used in the New Testament:

> Grace is the empowering presence of God, enabling you
> to become what God created you to become, and do what
> God calls you to do.

The Holy Spirit used this teaching in my life as a fresh reminder that God's plan for my life includes not only what I *do* but what I *become*. Under the Spirit's leadership, doing the Father's will always has imbedded within it the deeper purpose of conforming us to the character of Jesus.

This teaching also reminded me that the Spirit comes not only to teach and to lead, but also to *empower*.

For a time, the single word *grace* stood like a sentinel over my thought life. Dozens of times a day it reminded me that God's empowering presence was at work, enabling me to *become* what He created me to become and to *do* what He was calling me to do. It put wings on the call to know and follow God's plan for my life.

Consider another example, one that can be crucial. In the life of faith, the battle with spiritual enemies begins at the threshold of the mind. That is why Scripture puts such strong emphasis on renewing the *mind*. The battle begins there.

The enemy of a *renewed* mind is an *UN*renewed mind. No matter how far we have traveled with the Lord, the temptation is always to fall back—first into old ways of thinking, then into old ways of living. The apostle Paul describes the old life as one in which we gratify the cravings of our sinful nature and follow its desires and thoughts (Ephesians 2:3). Instead of living with a continual awareness of our Captains' presence, we find ourselves entertaining a herd of unprofitable thoughts. They have one thing in common: they divert us from hearing, trusting, and obeying our Captains.

How do you handle thoughts that invade your mind, crowding aside your faith in the presence and authority of the triune God who indwells you?

Some years ago I had an insight or revelation in regard to the habits of my mind.[4] I saw that the devil had carved out a considerable playground in my thought life. What I discovered was this: You do not conquer unprofitable or ungodly thoughts by striving against them with your own wit or will or determination. Rather, you *turn those thoughts over to Jesus.* Trust Him to deal with ungodly or unprofitable thoughts. Meanwhile, you settle into the remembrance of His indwelling presence.

Imagine the case of a man who has had a habit of lust. He cannot sit down at a lunch counter without casting a furtive, lusting glance at the waitress. He never goes by a newsstand without paging through some lascivious book or magazine. Even in his relations with his wife, there is more lust than tender love.

Then he receives the life of Christ. He knows that he cannot continue to do this sort of thing. But he does not at first understand how Jesus Christ and the Holy Spirit mean to lead him through this particular stretch in his life journey. So he merely applies the law. He tries to "contain" this lust of the flesh by his own resolve and willpower. He has a measure of success, but also many a failure. And in none of this is he really bound to Jesus in love. He may even begin inwardly to resent the hard life Jesus calls him to and excuse himself a little lusting.

But then he learns the truth of God's indwelling presence. When he sees a lewd magazine on a bus station rack, he does not fight against the temptation. He does not simply grit his teeth and suffer through it, saying over and over to himself, "I will not lust, I will not lust, I will not lust." Evil resisted grows stronger. "The power of sin is the law" (1 Corinthians 15:56). The more he invokes the law against his lusting, the more powerful grows the sin within him. He has tried that method before, and failed.

Instead, he meets the temptation at the doorway of his mind and says, "You'll have to take it up with Jesus. He's in charge."

He averts his eyes from the immediate source of temptation and reminds himself of Jesus' presence. It can be helpful to have a "replacement thought" at the ready. Perhaps he sings a hymn to himself. He praises Jesus in a joyful, confident spirit knowing that Jesus took the full measure of lust on the Cross. Jesus is a Captain with authority, well able to pilot him through this dangerous stretch of rapids.

As the man binds himself to Jesus in this conscious act of worship, the temptation will retreat. It is not the law that has saved him. He has simply turned the thing over to Jesus through an act of worship—a step of faith. He has reminded himself that the Captain of his journey is in charge; handling these intruding thoughts is His business.

Oswald Chambers points out how the active leadership of Jesus Christ differs from a human method or formula: Jesus says, "In that day you will ask in my name . . ." that is, in my nature. Not—"You will use my name as some magic word," but—"You will be so intimate with me that you will be one with me" (John 16:26).[5]

The Spirit's ways are many and varied. Over time, God will give you a variety of tools, or handles, to remind yourself of His indwelling presence. He may quicken a Bible verse, such as, "Be still, and know that I am God" (Psalm 46:10). This Scripture became a kind of watchword for the women's prayer group led for many years in our congregation by Jean Hahn. It helped a group of busy, often harried young mothers to structure into the middle of every week a time of quiet in which they reminded themselves of the Lord who watched over them and led them day by day.

Helmut Nicklas, a leader of spiritual renewal throughout Germany and the world, shared with my wife and me how his attitude toward God's will was reshaped by reminding himself many times a day, "I *delight* to do Your will, O my God" (Psalm 40:8 NKJV).

The Lord may give you a simple phrase like, "Let go, and let God," one of the phrases popularized by the deeper life movement. He may give you a mental image of a descending dove, or remind you of a scene from the Bible, such as Jesus walking beside the Sea of Galilee and saying to Simon and Andrew, "Come, follow me" (Mark 1:17). He may give you a symbolic image or a scene from your own life that reminds you of His faithfulness. He may give you a line from a hymn or a poem, or a well-phrased truth.

Symbols or works of art—hanging a religious picture or icon in your study, wearing a cross, listening to sacred music—are yet other means the Spirit may use to help remind you of God's empowering presence.

In time, the mere thought of the Holy Trinity living within you may sing into your thoughts like a lovely recurring grace note. Oswald Chambers describes the "final stage of the life of faith" as a time when "all of your commonsense decisions are actually God's will for you, unless you sense a feeling of restraint brought on by a check in your spirit."[6] The Spirit knows us intimately. He knows what can move us, and help us, at each stage of our journey.

It is important to realize that the words or images you use to remind yourself of God's empowering presence are not commands, telling you something you must do. On the contrary, they are reminders that you must *disengage*. They are tools, or helps, to turn your mind to God's presence.

Whatever tool of remembrance the Spirit may give you, let it serve as a reminder that the triune God is truly present and active in your life. He knows what to do and when to do it. You can give yourself over to His leadership. His initiative and timing may be different from yours, but that simply underscores the fact that He is the leader, you the follower.

The immediate sense that accompanies an act of remembrance is not usually of movement or of action, but of *stopping*. When you disengage from the pressure of your own thoughts and plans, consciously reminding yourself of the indwelling presence of the triune God, you will not necessarily experience anything special; nothing particular will happen. An act of remembrance is not a lever of action or power, but a step of faith—faith in the presence and purpose of the divine Captains who are in charge of your journey. What you are "remembering" is not how to do or accomplish something, but rather who is in charge. In an act of remembrance, you turn afresh to the leadership of Jesus Christ and the Holy Spirit.

Living with a vivid sense of the indwelling presence of the Lord is more than a mental habit. It is a reality, a living relationship that grows in intensity and effect *the more you call it to remembrance.*

As our awareness of the presence of the triune God increases, becoming the firm backdrop for the way we think about life and respond to practical situations, divine guidance rises to a new level. We move beyond occasional situations of searching uncertainly for a word or direction from God. We push beyond the boundary of only difficult choices or major decisions. The various ways that Jesus Christ and the Holy Spirit speak to us (see chapter 6) become our experience in everyday life. We wake each morning to the confident awareness that our divine Captains are at hand. Following them, we will Ride the River of the Father's plan for this day in our life journey.

Here Lies the Answer

It is worth recalling again the great secret, or mystery, of the Christian faith, according to the apostle Paul: "The mystery that has been kept hidden for ages and generations, but is now disclosed to the saints. To them God has chosen to make known . . . the glorious riches of this mystery, which is *Christ in you*, the hope of glory" (Colossians 1:26–27).

If we lament the feeble state of the Christian faith, in our own experience or in the church, we stand here before its chief cause: the indwelling presence of the triune God has been ignored, or "choked by life's worries, riches, and pleasures" (Luke 8:14). Whether for lack of teaching or because of self-chosen pursuits, whether consciously or unconsciously, we have frittered away our God-given freedom. We have gone where our own will and judgment have led us rather than welcoming the active leadership of Jesus Christ and the Holy Spirit.

Recurring remembrance of the indwelling presence of the Holy Trinity lifts you to a different level of life and living—not a place where problems disappear and instant blessings flow in abundance, but, paradoxically, a place where you recognize the hand of God even in the midst of suffering, the forward movement of God's plan despite difficulty and discouragement.

The men who signed on with Lewis and Clark knew that the journey would not be easy. Yet over and over again, in Lewis and Clark's journals, they record how cheerful the men were despite the hardships they had to endure. If they woke each morning hearing the voices of the captains, they knew that things were as they should be; they were ready to proceed on. Their one concern was to stick with their captains and complete the journey that President Jefferson had set for them.

Similarly, we will encounter times of trial that tempt us to turn aside from following our Captains. Then we need to remind ourselves: Our God is greater than any trouble we encounter. "Though the fig tree does not blossom, nor fruit be on the vines, the produce of the olive fail and the fields yield no food, the flock be cut off from the fold and there be no herd in the stalls, yet I will rejoice in the Lord, I will joy in the God of my salvation. God, the Lord, is my strength; he makes my feet like hinds' feet, he makes me tread upon my high places" (Habakkuk 3:17–19 RSV).

The recurring remembrance of God's indwelling presence reminds us that the Lord is in charge; things are as they should be. It brings us into a place best characterized, perhaps, by the biblical word *peace*. "Thou dost keep him in perfect peace *whose mind is stayed on thee*" (Isaiah 26:3 NKJV).

I have known the doctrine of the Holy Trinity as a "truth" for as long as I can remember. In the congregation where I grew up, the opening hymn every Sunday was—

> Holy, holy, holy, Lord God Almighty,
> Early in the morning our song shall rise to Thee;
> Holy, holy, holy, merciful and mighty
> God in Three Persons, Blessed Trinity!

That truth, however, gathered dust in a corner of my mind for many years. As far as I can see, it had little if any effect in my everyday life. But then God graciously brought this truth to life for me, reminding me again and again of His indwelling presence.

The experience has not been laden with great feeling or emotion. It has been more a sense of rest, of quiet confidence in the plan of the Father and the leadership of Jesus Christ and the Holy Spirit. A hundred times a day, or more, as I step into conscious remembrance that my life is indwelt by the living presence of the Holy Trinity, there comes a sense of release, of disengaging from the pressure of the moment, of giving up the impulse to initiate my own course of thinking or action, and settling into the awareness that Jesus Christ and the Holy Spirit know exactly what is going on, and where they want to lead me.

CHAPTER EIGHT
THE HOMECOMING

The leadership of the Captains makes it possible, one day, to give a good account of our life journey.

ON THEIR RETURN, as the Corps of Discovery traveled toward St. Louis, their joy and anticipation broke all bounds. Paddling downstream, they sometimes covered a hundred miles in a single day. They met trading parties, heading upstream, almost daily. One of them was led by John McClallen, an old friend that Lewis had known in the army. McClallen told them that dire rumors and speculations had circulated widely concerning their fate. Among them was the rumor that everyone in the expedition had been killed; another, that the Spanish had captured them and were working them as slave labor in the mines. McClallen informed them that they had long since been given up by the people of the United States and almost forgotten, though "the President had yet hopes of us."

On September 22, 1806, as they neared St. Louis, they gave a salute with their guns. The whole town gathered at the riverfront to welcome them back. They had traversed an uncharted wilderness for twenty-eight months, covering eight thousand miles (with the navigational instruments included in their supplies, they calculated the distance of the entire journey to within sixty miles!). They had accomplished the commission given them by President Thomas Jefferson.

Reporting to the President

The Christian life points beyond this life and this world to the kingdom of heaven (see 1 Corinthians 15:19). The Bible portrays scenes where believers are presented before the throne of God and give an account of their life (2 Corinthians 5:10; Matthew 25:34).

Lewis and Clark traveled from St. Louis to Washington, together with Sergeant Patrick Gass and several other members of the Corps of Discovery and a delegation of Indian leaders. On New Year's Day, 1807, they were received by President Jefferson.

We do not know what any member of the Corps of Discovery may have reported to President Jefferson. In bringing our parable to a close, we can imagine Sergeant Gass being invited to say some words on behalf of the Corps of Discovery. He was a plainspoken man, understandably nervous, yet he was secure in his relationship with Lewis and Clark through the long months of the expedition.

"It was quite a journey, Mr. President. It wasn't easy. We had some close calls. But the captains—Mr. President, the captains never let us down. I have to admit, we didn't always think they was right, like when we came to the fork of the Missouri and the Marias Rivers and didn't know which one was the real Missouri— well, they proved right even when all of us thought they was wrong.

"And, Mr. President, they showed us how to get along. Captain Lewis and Captain Clark, they always respected one another. I remember the time a couple of us got into a quarrel about some dumb thing. The captains never said a word to us, not a word. But when we sat around the fire that night, and just saw them sitting there cross-legged talking with each other so friendly and respectful, it shamed us right proper. They was so good to each other, it just showed us how we ought to be.

"Yes sir, they showed such respect for each other. They cared for each other. They really did love and look out for each other. Why, Mr. President, when Captain Lewis got shot in the butt— excuse me, Mr. President, but that's right where the bullet went—

it was an accident, but it was a real close call. Well, Captain Lewis he was laid up pretty bad for some days, and Captain Clark, he just nursed him and took care of him like a mother.

"They took care of us, too; took real good care. Some of us took pretty sick along the way. Well, they doctored us and kept us going. Sergeant Floyd, he died there early out from bad sickness, but he was the only one. From Mandan to the Pacific and back, we stuck together, Mr. President. Not a one of us was lost.

"The captains, they was brave, but they was cool-headed too. They made the right decisions.

"And they never let us forget what you sent us out there to do. They never let us forget that we was following out your orders, Mr. President. They led us the way you wanted and expected them to, and we came through. Yes sir, we came through, just the way you planned it, Mr. President. Because of them, we came through. We did what you sent us out to do.

"Mr. President, we rode the river!"

Glory be to the Father
  and to the Son,
  and to the Holy Spirit:
as it was in the beginning,
  is now,
  and ever shall be,
world without end. Amen.

—Gloria Patri

APPENDIX ONE

EXTENDED COMMENT ON THE DOCTRINE OF THE TRINITY

The doctrine points back to the experience.

ONE OF THE TRADITIONAL "handles" that theologians have used in connection with the doctrine of the Trinity is a phrase that says, "The operations of God *outward* are undivided, those *inward* are divided."[1] In other words, the reality of three persons in the Godhead belongs to the inner life of God; when God moves outward (toward man, for example), He is undivided, or one.

There is a clear sense in which this theological slogan is true: the Bible reveals three divine persons, but not much detail about intrapersonal relations within the Godhead; when God addresses man, He speaks for himself, and He speaks as one.

However, Scripture also presents the matter in another way. The triune identity of God is not exclusively a secret about God's inner life. It is also the way that people have actually experienced Him as He has moved outward, toward man, in history.

The Doctrine of the Trinity Is Rooted in Experience

The *doctrine* of the Trinity grew out of the *experience* Jesus' disciples had, that God is three, yet one. They grew up believing the creed of Israel, "Hear, O Israel: The Lord our God, the Lord is one" (Deuteronomy 6:4). Yet Jesus so identified himself with God that the disciples came to believe that He also was God. When He returned to heaven, He told them that "*another* Counselor" would come, the Holy Spirit, who would be with them forever.

The Holy Spirit came on the Day of Pentecost. The disciples also experienced the Spirit as God-present-with-us. The three persons of the Trinity were thus rooted in their experience.

Lutheran theologian Robert Jenson and Oxford scholar Alister McGrath both make the point that the name of the Trinity as "Father, Son, and Holy Spirit," and the resulting doctrine, is not essentially a philosophical concept; it is a shorthand summary of the way that God has revealed himself in history, according to the Christian scriptures of the Old and New Testament.

Jenson writes, " 'Father, Son, and Holy Spirit' became the church's name for its God because it packs into one phrase the content and logic of this God's identifying descriptions. These in turn embody the church's primal experience of God."[2]

McGrath makes the same point: "The doctrine of the Trinity wasn't *invented*—it was *uncovered*. . . . [It] is a summary of the Christian's answer to who God is and what he is like. [It] is the end result of a long process of thinking about the way in which God is present and active in the world."[3]

Two Misconceptions About the Trinity

Over the centuries, teachers in the church have sought to steer clear of two dangers in regard to the doctrine of the Trinity. On one side is the ditch of "tri-theism" (usually, *tritheism*), the danger that we end up worshiping three Gods instead of one. On the other side is the ditch that theologians call "subordinationism," the danger that we regard the Son and/or the Spirit as subordinate, or inferior, to God the Father, rather than coequal.

The way that Scripture itself presents the persons of the Trinity could tilt an individual toward either, or both, of these misconceptions. In the appendix to David Pawson's *The Normal Christian Birth*, he points out "that the apostolic writers themselves are open to the charge [of tritheism]. . . . It is a fact that, historically, the apostles came to a relationship with the three divine Persons at separate times."[4]

When Jesus was on earth, people encountered Him as a person, in the modern sense of that term. Jesus, in turn, spoke of the heavenly Father, and related to Him, in highly personal terms, particularly in prayer. Then Jesus introduced the Holy Spirit as "*another* Counselor," that is, Someone like himself, yet distinct from himself.

The New Testament shows people experiencing all three persons of the Godhead. The book you are now reading emphasizes the distinctiveness of each person of the Trinity and the desirability, indeed *necessity*, of personal encounter with each of the divine persons.

In theory, this emphasis could tilt an individual toward tritheism, relating to three different Gods. In practice, we have not found it so. Scripture balances its emphasis on the three divine persons not by downplaying the experience of the early church, but with the paradoxical assertion that God is, nevertheless, one. Jesus said, "I and the Father are one" (John 10:29). The apostle James wrote, "You believe that there is one God. Good!" (James 2:19; see also Revelation 19:20).

With good reason, the Bible shows believers in the early church having distinct experiences with each of the divine persons. It is a necessary dimension in discipleship. It is the thesis of this book that the empowering presence of God, and the divine guidance that flows from it, rests on the foundation of a vital relationship with all three persons of the Trinity.

The vibrant experience of the early church needs to be recaptured by the church in the twenty-first century. In everyday life and experience, believers need to encounter each of the persons of the Holy Trinity.

The Trinity: Unity and Diversity

Scripture characterizes the relationship between the divine persons in hierarchical terms. Jesus said, "The Father is greater than I" (John 14:28). Speaking of the Holy Spirit, Jesus said, "He will not speak on his own; He will speak only what he hears" (John 16:13). Standing alone, this could tilt a person toward the danger opposite to tritheism, the danger of subordinating Jesus and the Holy Spirit to the Father. The danger is more apparent than real; it is a subordination of *function*, not of *standing* or *worth*. The hierarchical structure is integral to the expression both of the *unity* and the *diversity* of the Holy Trinity.

In himself, God is radically and absolutely *one*, yet radically and absolutely *three*. No amount of mental gymnastics can resolve the mystery that God is one, yet three. Scripture lets the two truths stand side by side, an intellectual paradox.

At the practical level, however, the paradox is less daunting. Scripture presents God in a way that makes it possible for people to relate to Him and follow Him. On the one hand, Scripture *reveals* God in three persons, inviting personal relationship with or through each of the persons, as we note above.

At the level of human conception, and in view of relationship, the three persons in God predominate. We think of God as three, and radically so. There is no mixing or confusing of the three persons; each remains distinct.

On the other hand, Scripture *declares* that God is nevertheless one, curbing any tendency to rank or separate the persons. At the level of finding and following God's will, living out one's life in obedience to God, the unity in God never comes into question. Any relationship with or through one of the persons is a relationship with the living God, who is unshakably one.[5]

The Imago Dei: Scripture's Primary Clue Regarding the Trinity

When God wanted to put something on earth that was like himself, He created man *in His own image*. The *Imago Dei* ("image of God") is Scripture's primary clue to what God is like. Swiss Reformed theologian Karl Barth noted that this interpretation was widely held in the early church.[6]

Robert Jenson writes: "The triune identities [Father, Son, Holy Spirit] are not 'persons' in the modern sense. God [however] is [a person, in the modern sense]. If each identity is God, then each identity is also personal, and the three [are] a community."[7] Jenson is right in what he affirms, that the three divine persons constitute a community. When he says that the divine persons are not "persons" in the modern sense, however, he tilts away from the New Testament record, where believers experienced Father, Son, and Holy Spirit as distinct "persons" (though admittedly as Spirit persons, not human persons. See chapter 4).

The "image of God" embodies a further important implication: the category of *family* represents a reality in God. When God wanted to create something like himself, he created a man and a woman, a human family. *"Family" is Scripture's most profound image for linking together the concepts of UNITY and DIVERSITY.* Both unity and diversity are necessary to a trinitarian understanding of who God is and how we relate to Him.

In everyday life, we may relate to, or focus, now on one person of the Trinity, now on another. It is something like a well-adjusted child who relates now to his mother, now to his father, yet never to one apart from (or against!) the other. The differentness and the unity of Father, Son, and Holy Spirit is echoed in the differentness and the unity of a husband and a wife. (This is drawn out more explicitly in chapter 3.)

In the Lewis and Clark story we see something similar to *family*. Jefferson was a father figure to Lewis, who lived like a son in the White House, as Jefferson's personal secretary. Clark fully shared Lewis's commitment to Jefferson. They were three distinct persons, yet in regard to the Voyage of Discovery, the three were unconditionally united.

For the Corps of Discovery, it was self-evident, practical, and no mystery at all: Lewis, Clark, and, behind them, President Jefferson, spoke with one voice.

Appendix Two

Extended Comment on Receiving the Holy Spirit

When Jesus finished His life on earth, it marked, for His disciples, not an end but a transition. They would no longer see Him; He would not be physically present with them. Yet neither would He be absent from them. In following out the plan of God the Father, the disciples would become witnesses for Jesus to the ends of the earth (Acts 1:8). In this journey of faith and obedience, Jesus himself promised to be with them. "I will not leave you as orphans," He had promised. "I will come to you" (John 14:18). His parting words were, "Surely I am with you always, to the very end of the age" (Matthew 28:20).

But this was only half the promise. Another divine leader, the Holy Spirit, would also make the journey with them. In His final evening with them before His crucifixion, Jesus repeated this promise five times (John 14:16–17; 14:26; 16:7–11; 16:13–15).

Here more than anywhere else lies the uniqueness of the Christian faith. It is not a mere system of belief, nor a code of behavior, of which the world has produced many. The Christian faith gives rise to an altogether different kind of *life*, an existence that follows the will and purpose of God under the very present, indwelling leadership of Jesus Christ and the Holy Spirit.

The Prophecy of John the Baptist

John the Baptist testified: "I saw the Spirit come down from heaven as a dove and remain on [Jesus]. I would not have known him, except that the one who sent me to baptize with water told me, 'The man on whom you see the Spirit come down and remain is he who will baptize with the Holy Spirit.' I have seen and I testify that this is the Son of God" (John 1:32–34; see also Matthew 3:11, Mark 1:8, Luke 3:16).

Jesus repeated this prophecy on the day of His ascension—that His followers would be baptized with the Holy Spirit (Acts 1:5).

On the Day of Pentecost, Jesus baptized 120 of His followers with the Holy Spirit. When a crowd gathered, Peter stood up and told them that Jesus had "received from the Father the promised Holy Spirit and has poured out what you now see and hear." He went on to say, "Repent and be baptized, every one of you, in the name of Jesus Christ for the forgiveness of your sins. And you will receive the gift of the Holy Spirit. The promise is for you and your children and for all who are far off—for all whom the Lord our God will call" (Acts 2:33, 38–39). Many in the crowd repented, believed in the Lord Jesus, were baptized, received the gift of the Holy Spirit, and joined the fellowship of the apostles—three thousand of them in all.

The book of Acts records this happening in the lives of other (new) believers as the faith spread out. Several terms, virtually synonymous, are used to describe the happening: "receiving the Holy Spirit" (Acts 8:17), "being filled with the Holy Spirit" (Acts 2:4; 9:17), "receiving the gift of the Holy Spirit" (Acts 2:38; 10:45), "being baptized with the Holy Spirit" (Acts 1:5; 11:16).

A "Release" of the Holy Spirit?

One way of interpreting Jesus' ministry of baptizing people with the Holy Spirit operates around the word *release*. This approach presumes that the Holy Spirit comes as "part of the package" when a person becomes a Christian. What the Bible calls "receiving the Holy Spirit" or "being baptized in the Holy Spirit" happens when a person becomes a Christian; it needs only to be released in one's experience.

This way of looking at the matter has a certain initial appeal. It assumes that the way we are doing things is basically sound. If the power of the Holy Spirit appears to be weak or absent in a person's life, we simply exhort him to call it into action, to start using it: "You already have it. It needs only to be released!"

The inevitable companion of this idea is the belief that one may—and many do—receive the Holy Spirit unconsciously, secretly, in a hidden way. At some point later in time, one needs to become more conscious of the Spirit's presence; one then experiences a release of the Spirit. This has been spelled out with some precision, particularly by theologians in sacramental and evangelical traditions.

This approach, however, presents a nettlesome problem: Scripture gives no example of an unconscious receiving of the Holy Spirit. Whenever the New Testament records an instance of people receiving the Holy Spirit, it is always a conscious experience. (See appendix 4, "Extended Comment on the 'Release' of the Holy Spirit.")

A Second Receiving of the Holy Spirit?

Classical Pentecostalism recognized this discrepancy and came up with another way of explaining how the Holy Spirit becomes more active in a person's life. Their explanation operates around the word *second* or *subsequent*. They speak of two receptions of the Holy Spirit: one for a person's salvation; then a second, subsequent, reception to empower one for service, answering to the biblical term of being "baptized in the Holy Spirit."[1]

The Pentecostal doctrine of baptism with the Holy Spirit as "a second work of grace" had its roots in the Holiness Movement of the nineteenth century.[2]

This approach is hard to reconcile with the plain sense of the biblical text. In Acts, to be "baptized with the Holy Spirit" (Acts 1:5; 11:15–17) means the same as to "receive the Holy Spirit" (Acts 8:14–17).[3] The term "receive the Holy Spirit" is not used to describe two different actions of the Holy Spirit—one to accomplish salvation, then a second receiving to equip one for ministry or service. It shows people taking distinct steps that bring them into a life of discipleship to Jesus Christ; "receiving the Holy Spirit" (or "being baptized with the Holy Spirit") is one of the steps.

Jesus' encounter with some of His disciples on Easter evening is sometimes cited as a text in which "receiving the Holy Spirit" may refer to salvation. Jesus said, "Peace be with you! As the Father has sent me, I am sending you. And with that he breathed on them and said, 'Receive the Holy Spirit' " (John 20:21–22). In this text, Jesus seems to be speaking and acting "proleptically," that is, pointing to something yet future. He was preparing the disciples for what would happen at Pentecost. Jesus had not yet ascended to heaven: Scripture indicates that the Holy Spirit would not actually be given until Jesus had been glorified (John 7:39; Acts 2:33). (For a thorough discussion of John 20:21–22, see Pawson, *Jesus Baptises in One Holy Spirit*, 65–70.)

The Biblical Pattern

A more recent approach by David Pawson takes the biblical pattern as it stands. Pawson's work, particularly his careful interpretation of the biblical texts, offers a straightforward approach to the question of how Jesus baptizes people with the Holy Spirit.

In the foreword to Pawson's *Jesus Baptises in One Holy Spirit*, Dr. Mark Stibbe acknowledges how Pawson's work caused him to modify what he had previously written on the subject of Spirit baptism: "I [had shown] that the word *baptise* comes from the Greek verb *baptizo* which literally means 'to saturate entirely'. Having said that, I then made the mistake of opting for what David Pawson calls the 'time-bomb' theory of Spirit baptism. In other words, I proposed two things: first, that it is possible, when we are converted, to be baptised in the Holy Spirit without realising it; second, that the full realisation of this experience can happen later as the Spirit, given at our conversion-initiation, is 'released' in power at a later date. David immediately spotted the inconsistency here. He expressed his critique in the following way: 'If baptism in the Holy Spirit is "an intensive, immersive, and invasive experience", how can it happen without the recipient knowing that it's happened?'

"I want to nail my colours firmly to the mast and say that I agree wholeheartedly with what David says on p. 195: that sacramentalists need to distinguish clearly between baptism in water and baptism in the Holy Spirit; evangelicals need to distinguish clearly between believing in Jesus and receiving the Holy Spirit; and that pentecostals need to relinquish the view that there are two receptions of the Spirit. What we need today is a comprehensive view of conversion-initiation which comprises repentance of sin, faith in Christ, water baptism, and receiving the gift of the Holy Spirit in power."

Pawson's work operates around the word *receive*. He uses the word as Scripture does, to describe one particular thing that happens in connection with becoming a Christian.

According to the biblical pattern, receiving the Spirit is one link in the chain of experience that draws a person into the life of Christian discipleship. (The other "links," according to our metaphor: repentance toward God, believing in Jesus, baptism in water, becoming part of the Christian fellowship.) What the Bible calls "receiving the Holy Spirit" does not happen unconsciously, or automatically, in connection with some other link in the chain—such as baptism, or believing in Jesus. Nor are there two "receivings" of the Holy Spirit, one for salvation, another for power and service.

Like each of the other links, receiving the Spirit has its particular focus and purpose: the Spirit draws closer; one has a more intimate experience of His presence, of His working and His power in one's life.

What the Bible calls "receiving the Holy Spirit" is as distinct and as necessary as repentance, believing in the Lord Jesus, baptism in water, and becoming part of the fellowship of believers. *If it is missing in a person's experience, it needs to be made up.*

What Happens When a Person Receives the Holy Spirit?

The following comment of Jacob Tanner, a Lutheran theologian of an earlier generation, is particularly instructive because it was not affected by doctrinal controversies between Pentecostalism and its opponents, but rests simply on his interpretation of the biblical text. It comes close to stating the Pentecostal view of the relationship between baptism with the Spirit and speaking in tongues: "This baptizing with the Spirit . . . was not a baptism unto salvation, but a baptism unto work. Its most noticeable manifestation was the speaking with other tongues. In fact, it was the ability to speak with other tongues that furnished the proof that the Holy Spirit had, in a special way, fallen upon one."[4]

"Speaking in other *languages*" would be a more normal translation of this Greek term, yet the term "speaking in tongues" serves well to convey an important aspect of its meaning: In the New Testament, "speaking in tongues" is a technical term for a spiritually or religiously effected utterance, a peculiar language, that is, a "language of the Spirit."[5]

The Pentecostal teaching that speaking in tongues is the "initial evidence" that a person has been baptized with the Holy Spirit has provoked considerable debate. Pentecostals may push Scripture too far, saying that speaking in tongues is the only initial evidence of Spirit baptism.

Their opponents, however, who dismiss the idea of evidence altogether, or cite virtually anything at random (love, mercy, unity, peace, justice) as the "*real* evidence of having received the Holy Spirit," or theologize tongues away by one means or another are clearly off target.

The most common way to theologize speaking in tongues out of existence has been in the context of "dispensational theology." It argues that tongues were a temporary expedient to help jump-start the New Testament church. Once the church was established tongues were no longer necessary and "would cease" (so its selective reading of 1 Corinthians 13:8). Once the canon of Scripture was established, the church entered a new dispensation in which different ground rules apply.

Other attempts to theologize away the plain meaning and purpose of tongues can follow virtually any predisposition that a theologian may have. For example, Robert Jenson writes: "The eschatological [having to do with the end times or the age to come] power of the Spirit breaks through all argument. All creation is a mere present from God for the Child and children (Romans 8:17–18). Therefore it waits—or rather, cannot wait—precisely for us. Though we cannot understand it, this waiting too is verbal (vv. 19–22). The prayers of creation, *perhaps the only true and necessary 'speaking in tongues'* are the Spirit's, that is, they too are prophecy" [emphasis added].[6] Such fanciful interpretations find no support in the text of Scripture. The Holy Spirit will certainly work changes in a person's virtue and behavior; all His work is worthy of serious theological reflection. None of this, however, was what people "heard" and "saw" when people received the Holy Spirit in the book of Acts. They witnessed something that immediately arrested their attention—people breaking forth in spontaneous speech, as Pawson accurately notes.

Dealing With Problems

The idea of receiving the Holy Spirit may evoke an understandable defensiveness with some people.

David Pawson poses some of the most common objections: "Are you saying that I don't have the Holy Spirit, that I'm not a Christian? That I shouldn't be member of this church? That I'm not saved? That I won't go to heaven when I die?"[7]

The question is not whether a person is a Christian, but whether people who *are* Christians need to make up things that are missing in their experience. Nevertheless, this kind of response is understandable if people have been taught that they receive the Holy Spirit more or less automatically, along with baptism or conversion. "If every Christian already 'has' the Holy Spirit, why do I need to 'receive' the Holy Spirit?"

We pointed out in chapter 4 that the Holy Spirit did many things in the lives of Jesus' disciples before they received the Holy Spirit on the Day of Pentecost. Also, in Samaria, He brought new believers to faith in Christ, and they were baptized; they did not receive the Holy Spirit until Peter and John specifically prayed for them to receive.

The Holy Spirit is active in the lives of many Christians today. The teaching about "receiving the Holy Spirit" or "baptism with the Holy Spirit" does not take away, or downgrade, anything that the Holy Spirit has already done and is still doing in the life of a believer. But having the Holy Spirit with you and active in your life is not identical with what the Bible calls "receiving the Holy Spirit."

In His sovereignty and mercy, God allows the Holy Spirit to work in people's lives and ministries, sometimes with great effect, despite some lack in their teaching or experience. In the book of Acts, we see something like this in the case of Apollos: "He was a learned man, with a thorough knowledge of the Scriptures. He had been instructed in the way of the Lord, and he spoke with great fervor and taught about Jesus accurately, though he knew only the baptism of John." Two of Paul's co-workers, Priscilla and Aquilla, heard Apollos; they "invited him to their home and explained to him the way of God more adequately" (Acts 18:24–26). Priscilla and Aquilla did not dispute with Apollos or downgrade his ministry. They simply helped him make up something that was lacking. They could affirm his ministry without allowing a lack in his teaching and experience to bypass something that the Holy Spirit wanted him to have.

God may bless and work mightily in the life of a person who has not been baptized in water. That does not mean that we should enshrine nonbaptism as a new practice for the church. The same logic applies with regard to receiving the Holy Spirit. To take someone's experience—or *lack* of experience!—and make it a new norm for the Christian life because God has blessed that person creates more problems than it solves. Scripture is our only reliable standard.

Actually, the language of "release," preferred by some, and the language of "receive," which I advocate, may not end up all that far apart in practice. Who can look at the state of the church today and not lament the woeful lack of the power of the Holy Spirit? One person may say, "We need a *release* of the Holy Spirit, who is within us." Another may say, "We need to *receive* the Holy Spirit, who has been promised." They read the present situation identically: the Holy Spirit needs to become more active in our lives. One sees this as a release of that which has been given, but which is dormant. The other sees it as receiving something that has been promised. Both descriptions have the same end in view: an increase of the presence and power of the Holy Spirit.

The language used to describe this aspect of Christian experience is still in flux. People may have a genuine encounter with the Holy Spirit, such as we are here considering, yet understand or describe it somewhat differently. God does not withhold His blessing until we cross all our theological *T*'s in the same way.

William Martin recounts a significant experience in the life of Billy Graham in his book *A Prophet with Honor: The Billy Graham Story*: "Stephen Olford [said], 'I gave [Billy Graham] my testimony of how God completely turned my life inside out—an experience of the Holy Spirit in His fullness and anointing. As I talked, and I can see him now, those marvelous eyes glistened with tears, and he said, "Stephen, I see it. That's what I want. That's what I need in my life." ' Olford suggested they 'pray this through', and both men fell on their knees. 'I can still hear Billy pouring out his heart in a prayer of total dedication to the Lord. Finally, he said, "My heart is so flooded with the Holy Spirit" and he went from praying to praising.

We were laughing and praising God and he was walking back and forth across the room, crying out, "I have it, I'm filled. This is the turning point in my life." And he was a new man.' "[8]

Billy Graham alludes to this in his autobiography: "My contact with British evangelical leaders during this and subsequent trips, especially with Stephen Olford, deepened my personal spiritual life."[9]

Billy Graham's experience was not unlike experiences reported by Christian leaders in earlier generations; for example, Dwight L. Moody, Hudson Taylor, and Charles Finney.[10]

The reality of the encounter is more important than the language used to describe it. Nevertheless, language that is as precise and close to the biblical description as possible may be more helpful to people who want to enter into the experience.

In some of my earlier writings I have used the language of "release" to describe the experience. It seemed to fit better with Lutheran theology. It steered around the heated objection that people without the experience are made to feel like "second-class Christians." As one man said, "The language of 'release' steps on fewer toes!"[11]

Two considerations, however, incline me to modify my earlier writings and now use the language of "receive." Foremost, I believe that it is more true and consistent to the plain meaning of the biblical texts. When Scripture describes people being baptized in the Holy Spirit, it portrays the Holy Spirit as "coming upon" them (Acts 10:44; 19:6). The appropriate response would be to "receive." Secondly, it puts primary focus upon the need for a personal relationship with the Holy Spirit; it does not assume that such a relationship is already present, fully in order, needing only to be manifested in outward ways. "Baptism with the Holy Spirit" has first of all to do with the *person* of the Holy Spirit, secondarily with what He will do in and through the life of a believer. Whether we conceive of Him sitting unrecognized in a corner of our life, or standing at the threshold, He needs to be *received*.

In terms of doctrine, the Holy Spirit has been recognized from earliest times as the third person of the Trinity, equal in glory and coequal in majesty with the Father and the Son. Yet ask any random sampling of Christians what place the Holy Spirit plays in their life—

how real He is in their own experience—and you will harvest a bumper crop of stuttering uncertainties.

In preparing His disciples to receive the Holy Spirit, Jesus said that the Spirit would be fully identified with Him (John 16:14) yet also distinct both from Him and from God the Father (John 14:6; 15:26). He presented God the Father to them in a similar way— identified with Jesus, yet also distinct from Him (John 14:8–11; 16:26–27). A personal relationship with the Holy Spirit is as possible, and as necessary, as a personal relationship with Jesus Christ or with God the Father (see John 14:23). *Receiving the Holy Spirit brings the fullness and balance of trinitarian Christianity into the life and experience of believers.*

EXTENDED COMMENT ON SPEAKING IN TONGUES

Is speaking in tongues the "initial evidence" that a person has received the Holy Spirit?

IN FEBRUARY 1993, Pentecostal historian Vinson Synan was preparing a *Festschrift* for Presbyterian theologian J. Rodman Williams. In gathering material, he asked me to give him my present view with regard to the question of speaking in tongues as initial evidence. I presented a position that would generally be held by Lutherans with firsthand experience in the Charismatic Renewal. The following comment is adapted from my letter to him:

> The first thing I ever published on speaking in tongues was the little booklet *Speaking in Tongues: A Gift for the Body of Christ.* It was mimeographed and re-mimeographed, printed up in several different editions, and distributed by various groups, both in English and foreign language translations; it received wide distribution in the early days of the Charismatic Renewal.
>
> In that booklet, I state, "Does [the assumption that the believers in Samaria spoke in tongues when they received the Holy Spirit] mean that everyone who receives the Holy Spirit will speak in tongues—and that if you have not spoken in tongues you have not really received the Holy Spirit? *I do not believe that you can make such a case from Scripture.*"[1]
>
> I would have the same understanding today. I recognize that speaking in tongues is mentioned in connection with every instance in Acts where charismatic manifestations of the Holy Spirit are reported in connection with people being baptized with the

Holy Spirit (Acts 2:4; 10:46; 19:6). Admittedly, the *every instance* argument carries some weight. Nevertheless, the evidence is anecdotal; lacking any definitive biblical commentary on these anecdotes or instances of speaking in tongues, one must address the question with a measure of caution.

The initial evidence argument runs into a further difficulty, it seems to me, in both of the later passages in Acts. In 10:46 (RSV) it says, ". . . they heard them speaking in tongues *and extolling God.*" In 19:6 it says, ". . . they spoke with tongues *and prophesied.*" Neither the grammar nor the context makes unmistakably clear whether the *and* in these two passages is distributive or inclusive, that is, whether (1) *some* spoke in tongues, while *others* extolled God/prophesied; or (2) whether all those present *both* spoke in tongues *and* extolled God/prophesied. Neither the initial evidence nor the contra-initial evidence argument has the better of it here. It's a standoff.

I do not believe that Paul's teaching on spiritual gifts in First Corinthians has any significant bearing on the question of initial evidence. He is primarily addressing the question of how gifts *that have been received* should be used. He does not directly address the question of whether or how one should receive a specific gift of the Holy Spirit, other than to admonish believers to "earnestly desire" [all] spiritual gifts.

It might be helpful to at least look at the question of initial evidence from another point of view. It seems abundantly evident that speaking in tongues has played a significant role in the spread both of the Pentecostal and Charismatic movements. I believe that Gerlach and Hine, together with Kilian McDonnell, concluded that neither movement would have spread without the catalytic role played by tongues.[2] The teaching of "tongues as initial evidence" may well have contributed to this.

This shifts the question of initial evidence to another arena. Instead of marshalling biblical evidence and arguments, we are asking another kind of question: "What significance or role has God assigned to speaking in tongues *in the present-day outpouring of the Holy Spirit?*" Theologically, it stands beyond question that God can use any of the gifts of the Holy Spirit when, where, and how He chooses to do so.

So the question is, *"Has God chosen to emphasize and use the gift of tongues in a special way, through the Pentecostal and Charismatic movements?"*

To answer this question with a resounding YES!! goes neither against nor beyond Scripture. We offer opinions, statements, and judgments about what we, in the light of Scripture, believe God may be doing in regard to any number of current situations. When I look back over more than thirty years of personal experience within the Charismatic Renewal, I must state my conviction that God has indeed assigned a special role and function to the gift of tongues. For many people, speaking in tongues serves as a gateway experience into the charismatic dimension, where the reality of the Holy Spirit begins to chart a new course in one's Christian commitment and discipleship.

One might package the distinction I am trying to make something like this:

- "*Must* I speak in tongues (is it biblically, theologically mandated) in order to receive the Holy Spirit or be filled with the Spirit?" Answer: No.
- "Does God *want* me to speak in tongues? Is it part of His plan and will for me in this present time?" Answer: Not unlikely.

So . . . you as a classical Pentecostal, and I as a Lutheran, may come at the question somewhat differently. Praise God, He blesses both of us with this *blessed gift*!

EXTENDED COMMENT ON THE "RELEASE" OF THE HOLY SPIRIT

THE FOLLOWING SUMMARIES show how different traditions have used the language of "release" to describe a believer's experience of the Holy Spirit. My own earlier use of this term is also cited on page 206. I have come to believe, however, that "release" is not the most accurate, or helpful, way to describe the experience, as I will point out.

The Orthodox View

The indwelling presence of the Holy Spirit is given to us "secretly," in such a way that we are not at first consciously aware of it. . . . God nevertheless awaits a response on our part; and if we fail to make that response, although the Spirit will still continue to be present "secretly" in our heart, we shall not feel His presence "actively" within us, nor experience His fruits with full conscious awareness. . . . Our starting-point is the presence of baptismal grace with us "secretly" and unconsciously; our end-point is the revelation of that grace "actively," with "full assurance and sensation. . . ." Our spiritual programme can therefore be summed up in the maxim "Become what you are."[1]

The Roman Catholic View

The reappropriation of initiation with the charisms, *which is baptism in the Holy Spirit*, offers a significant opportunity for life in Christ. . . . All are called to *fan into flame the gift of the Holy Spirit received in the sacraments of initiation*. God freely gives this grace, but it requires a personal response of ongoing conversion to the Lordship of Jesus Christ and openness to the transforming presence and power of the Holy Spirit."[2]

A Lutheran Perspective

In an earlier writing, I have said, "The Lutheran sees [baptism with the Holy Spirit] as a releasing of the Spirit which has already been given, for power and ministry. The 'spring of water' (John 4:14) becomes an 'outflowing river' (John 7:38). . . . In one sense every Christian has been 'baptized with the Spirit' inasmuch as he has received Christian Baptism in the name of the Father, Son, and Holy Spirit. In this sense baptism with the Holy Spirit belongs to the inheritance of every Christian. The term, however, is also used in an experiential sense. When used in this way it refers to the event or process by which the power of the Holy Spirit is *released* in a fresh way. In this sense baptism with the Holy Spirit is the Spirit being *actualized*, or coming to more conscious manifestation, in one's life."[3]

This same teaching, again in a Lutheran context, is succinctly expressed in an article by Delbert Rossin: "The Holy Spirit is *resident* in every Christian, but he wants to be *President*."[4]

The Problem of Special Pleading

When I wrote *The Charismatic Renewal Among Lutherans*, a Lutheran colleague asked me, "Are you trying to cram too much into a precast Lutheran theological mold?"

I have studied and reflected on the exegetical, theological, and practical implications of receiving the Holy Spirit for nearly forty years. I have sometimes compared the efforts to systematize the material in Acts to packing a suitcase. The sacramentalist pushes, crams, and squeezes, and finally snaps it shut—only to discover that a sock from chapter 10 is hanging out on one side. The evangelical comes along and offers to repack the suitcase. Push, cram, squeeze, *snap*—

but a pajama leg from chapter 8 is left hanging out the other side.

Each of the primary streams of interpretation must do a certain amount of "special pleading"—snip off something that doesn't quite fit in—when they try to pack "receiving the Holy Spirit" into their particular system. In other words, they must interpret this or that passage as a special case, dictated by the circumstances, as a way of explaining away the illustrative or paradigmatic value that a more natural reading of the text would give.

The eighth chapter of Acts has provided a classic case of special pleading for those who believe that people receive the Holy Spirit along with faith in Christ or along with baptism.

> Philip went down to a city in Samaria and proclaimed the Christ there. When the crowds heard Philip and saw the miraculous signs he did, they paid close attention to what he said. . . . When they believed Philip as he preached the good news of the kingdom of God and the name of Jesus Christ, they were baptized, both men and women. . . . When the apostles in Jerusalem heard that Samaria had accepted the word of God, they sent Peter and John to them. When they arrived, they prayed for them that they might receive the Holy Spirit, because the Holy Spirit had not yet come upon any of them; they had simply been baptized into the name of the Lord Jesus. Then Peter and John placed their hands on them, and they received the Holy Spirit. (Acts 8:5–17)

Three facts stand crystal clear in the text itself: people believed; they were baptized; they did not automatically receive the Holy Spirit.

The British evangelical James Dunn devotes an entire chapter to this text and titles it, "The Riddle of Samaria." In a speculative tour de force he contends that the Samaritans were not truly converted. When Peter and John came, they were truly converted and then they received the Holy Spirit. "Luke's aim is to highlight the difference between true and false Christianity."[5]

The interpretation of Presbyterian missionary theologian Frederick Bruner is even more contorted. He holds that the intent of the story is to teach "the divinely purposed and accomplished union of baptism in the name of Jesus Christ with the gift of the Holy Spirit apart from subjective conditions. The Spirit is temporarily suspended from Baptism 'only' and precisely to teach the church at its most prejudiced juncture, and in its strategic initial missionary move beyond Jerusalem, that *suspension cannot occur*. This is the New Testament's only record of Christian Baptism without the immediately present gift of the Christian Spirit, and the immediate resolution of this enormity, teaches in a most impressive but not unconfusing manner the New Testament's normative and important doctrine of the 'one baptism' of the church. Baptism in the name of Christ *cannot* but be baptism in the Holy Spirit; Christian Baptism cannot but be accompanied with the gift of the Holy Spirit [italics his]."[6] Broken down to plain language, Bruner says that God let this happen one time to show that it should never happen again!

The Roman Catholic New Testament scholar George Montague argues that the issue of apostolic authority plays a part in this event. "Philip's mission to Samaria was not commissioned by the apostles; he simply left Jerusalem because of persecution. The resulting turn of events raised a new question concerning the incorporation of this mission under the supervision of the apostles. The delay of the Spirit in Samaria, and its coming through the apostles Peter and John, permits Jesus' programmatic commissioning to be fulfilled. It was to the apostles, not to Philip, that Jesus had given the commission to witness 'in Jerusalem, throughout Judea and Samaria, and to the ends of the earth.' " Montague also pleads the unusualness of the Samaritan episode as it touches on baptism: "Luke certainly considers the Samaritan situation unusual, and therefore not one which sets a standard for Christian practice. It is not the normal situation that the dispositions of the recipient would be so defective as to nullify the effect of Baptism."[7]

The Plain Sense of Scripture

These efforts deal with significant issues, theologically and historically. All of them, however, must resort to special pleading when they interpret certain of the texts. None of them, including my own earlier writing, cited on page 206, is able to read all of the relevant Scriptures without resorting to special pleading.

At this point, Martin Luther's standard of exegesis is a good reminder for all students of Scripture: "Neither an inference nor a trope [a figure of speech that uses words in a nonliteral sense] is admissible in any passage of Scripture, unless it is forced on us by the evident nature of the context and the absurdity of the literal sense as conflicting with one or another of the articles of faith. *Instead, we must everywhere stick to the simple, pure, and natural sense of the words that accords with the rules of grammar and the normal use of language.* . . . Heresies and errors in connection with the Scriptures have arisen, not from the simplicity of the words, as is almost universally stated, but from neglect of the simplicity of the words, and from tropes or inferences hatched out of men's own heads."[8]

The plain sense of Scripture—particularly Acts 8:14–17—does not support the idea of a "hidden" or "unconscious" receiving of the Holy Spirit, which may be released at some later time. A person who comes to faith in Christ, and/or is baptized, does not automatically receive the Holy Spirit, in the sense that Scripture uses this term. The plain sense of Scripture does encourage believers to pray for, and receive, the gift of the Holy Spirit.

A distinction between "a *release* of the Holy Spirit" and "*receiving* the Holy Spirit" may in part be semantic. My concern, however, is *pastoral*. I ask the question, "How can we help people experience more of the Holy Spirit in their everyday lives?" What more natural and compelling way than inviting them to *receive* the Holy Spirit from Jesus, who baptizes with the Holy Spirit today as surely as He did that first Pentecost?

BIBLIOGRAPHY

In writing this book, I have drawn on a variety of resources. The titles listed below represent a select bibliography relating to some of the themes and background material in the book.

Christian Life and Growth

Oswald Chambers. *My Utmost for His Highest*. Grand Rapids, Mich.: Discovery House, 1992.

Andrew Murray. *The Spirit of Christ*. Minneapolis: Bethany House, 1979.

These are classic works of devotional literature. They offer many helpful insights on the reality, and effect, of the indwelling presence of the Holy Spirit in the life of a believer. Both of them include a number of specific comments on the theme of divine guidance.

Larry Christenson. *The Renewed Mind*. Minneapolis: Bethany House, 1974, 2001.

This book presents the theme of Christian life and growth through a series of stories, parables, and metaphors, emphasizing radical dependence on the presence of the Lord in the everyday life of a believer.

Prayer

Andrew Murray. *The Believer's School of Prayer*. Minneapolis: Bethany House, 1985.

O. Hallesby. *Prayer*. Minneapolis: Augsburg, 1994.

These two classics give biblical and practical teaching on building and maintaining a rich life of personal prayer.

Tricia McCary Rhodes. *The Soul at Rest*. Minneapolis: Bethany House, 1996.

This book offers excellent help for enhancing your quiet time with God through meditative prayer. It answers the busyness of life with practical helps for cultivating habits of quiet reflection and greater intimacy with God.

Larry Christenson. *The Christian Family*. Minneapolis: Bethany House, 1970.

The second part of this book, "Practicing the Presence of Jesus," is a practical handbook on developing prayer in the family.

Receiving the Holy Spirit and His Gifts

David Pawson. *The Normal Christian Birth*. London: Hodder & Stoughton, 1989.

David Pawson. *Jesus Baptises in One Holy Spirit*. London: Hodder & Stoughton, 1997.

Pawson presents a coherent and thought-provoking description (exegetically and theologically) of the process by which people became Christians in the early church. His interpretation of the New Testament import of "receiving the Holy Spirit," or "being baptized in the Holy Spirit," deals with this question in a comprehensive and helpful way.

Larry Christenson. *Speaking in Tongues*. Minneapolis: Bethany House, 1968, 1987.

This is a practical handbook on the value and use of the gift of "speaking in tongues." It also includes an appendix on developing a habit of personal prayer, "How to Have a Daily Quiet Time."

The Lewis and Clark Expedition

The basic historical facts of the Lewis and Clark expedition, and quotations from the journals of Lewis and Clark, are available from a variety of sources. I have not generally footnoted them in the text of this book.

Principal resources are listed below in the approximate order of importance that they had for my research. Where specific incidents from the journals are referenced in the endnotes, I list first the author (Lewis or Clark) and the date, then the specific edition from which a particular reference is taken. This enables a reader to locate references, even though one may have a different edition of the journals.

Stephen E. Ambrose. *Undaunted Courage: Meriwether Lewis, Thomas Jefferson, and the Opening of the American West.* New York: Touchstone, Simon & Schuster, 1996.

Historian Stephen Ambrose is widely regarded as the greatest living authority on the Lewis and Clark expedition. His excellently written work, Undaunted Courage, *is the best account and evaluation of the epic journey currently available.*

Bernard DeVoto, editor. *The Journals of Lewis and Clark.* New York: Houghton Mifflin Company, 1953, 1981.

Frank Bergon, editor. *The Journals of Lewis and Clark.* New York: Penguin Books, 1989, 1995.

Elliott Coues, editor. *History of the Expedition Under the Command of Lewis and Clark.* New York: Dover Publication, Inc., 1965, 1893.

Carol Lynn MacGregor, editor. *The Journals of Patrick Gass.* Missoula, Mont.: Mountain Press Publishing Company, 1997.

The DeVoto edition of the Lewis and Clark journals is generally considered the benchmark. Bergon's personal notes are often insightful. Coues' is an earlier edition of the journals, more detailed than any but the original Thwaites edition. The Patrick Gass journal offers the perspective of a member of the Corps of Discovery and occasional details not found in the Lewis and Clark journals.

Systematic and Practical Theology

Robert W. Jenson. *The Triune Identity*. Philadelphia: Fortress Press, 1982.

Alister E. McGrath. *Understanding the Trinity*. Grand Rapids, Mich.: Academie Books, Zondervan, 1988.

Jenson and McGrath both see the doctrine of the Trinity not primarily as a philosophical/theological concept, but as a description of God that reflects the experience of the early church.

Don Meares. *Grace: the Empowering Presence of God*. Six audio cassettes, published by Don Meares Ministry, 13901 Central Avenue, Upper Marlboro, Maryland 20774.

Bishop Meares shows that the central thrust of the New Testament meaning of grace is not simply "favor," but presence. God shows His favor by and through His empowering presence in the life of the believer.

Larry Christenson, editor. *Welcome, Holy Spirit: A Study of Charismatic Renewal in the Church*. Minneapolis: Augsburg Publishing, 1987.

Carl E. Braaten and Robert W. Jenson, editors. *Union with Christ: The New Finnish Interpretation of Luther*. Grand Rapids, Mich.: William B. Eerdmans Publishing Company, 1998.

Both of these books present faith as a union of the believer with the indwelling presence of Christ.

ENDNOTES

Chapter One

1. Alister E. McGrath, *Understanding the Trinity* (Grand Rapids, Mich.: Zondervan Publishing, 1988), 54–58. McGrath cautions that, in utilizing metaphors or models to talk about God, "it may be [falsely] assumed that something which is necessary for the model is also necessary for whatever is being modeled."
2. Stephen Ambrose, lecture at the Charles Russell Museum, Great Falls, Montana, 27 June 1997.
3. Frank Bergon, ed., *The Journals of Lewis and Clark* (New York: Penguin, 1989), xiii.
4. Harriet Crabtree, *The Christian Life: Traditional Metaphors and Contemporary Theologies* (Minneapolis: Fortress Press, 1991). "Of all the images, that of journey or pilgrimage is the hardest to present in short compass because every person who speaks of the Christian life as a journey, has in mind a journey of a slightly different kind. Their understandings of the journey are as varied as the stories and examples that have shaped their vision of what it means to travel through this earthly existence in the company of Christ, his people, and indeed of all the peoples of earth of generations past, present, and to come" (p. 131).

   Crabtree summarizes various traditional treatments of the journey image in Christian literature. The primary focus is almost invariably on the moral development or spiritual achievement of the one(s) making the journey.

   My use of the image includes this emphasis somewhat as a by-product, but focuses primarily on the journey as a description of God's plan for one's life and the adventure of finding and following the plan.

Crabtree concludes: " 'Pilgrimage,' and its more secular relation 'journey,' are likely to endure as guiding life-metaphors for mainstream Christians. They are biblically rooted, deeply embedded in the tradition, and congenial because of the way that their structures can reflect analogically the progress of the spirit. The question that confronts us is the one of how they are to be developed" (p. 161).

5. For some readers, casting specific human beings as the persons of the Trinity may be troublesome. The closest parallel from Scripture would be *typology*, where certain persons and events represent something about God. The prophet Hosea, for example, understood that his marriage mirrored something of the relationship between God and Israel. "The Lord said to me, 'Go, show your love to your wife again, though she is loved by another and is an adulteress. Love her as the Lord loves the Israelites, though they turn to other gods" (Hosea 3:1). A particular aspect of Hosea's life and experience was used to illustrate an important truth about God. Other aspects of Hosea's life were passed over in silence; they were not relevant to the typology.

In our parable, Jefferson, Lewis, and Clark represent the persons of the Holy Trinity, with particular reference to how They lead us in our life journey. Our interest in Jefferson, Lewis, and Clark focuses narrowly on how they led the Corps of Discovery in a journey of exploration through the American West. Other aspects of their lives play no part in the parable.

Some readers may find it difficult to accept the parable because of other things they know about these men. In his religious beliefs, for instance, Jefferson has generally been regarded as a deist, not an orthodox Christian. Though he wrote "all men are created equal" into the Declaration of Independence, he himself owned slaves. The allegation that he may have fathered a child by one of his slaves is unlikely, but not impossible ("Thomas Jefferson and Sally Hemmings," www.people.virginia.edu/rjh9u/tomsally.html). Clark was also a slave owner. His personal servant, York, made the journey as a full-fledged member of the Corps of Discovery, yet received none of the pay or benefits given to the other members. The death of Lewis was clouded in mystery. Stephen Ambrose believes that the evidence points to suicide.

Alongside such items you could of course list many things to admire in each of the men. For example, Jefferson's statesmanlike friendship and correspondence with John Adams, his lifelong political opponent; or

Lewis's high-minded resolve, on his thirty-first birthday, to live the remainder of his life *"for mankind* as I have heretofore lived *for myself"*; or Clark's generosity, when Sacagawea died in her mid-twenties, in taking her son Pomp, and a younger sister born after the journey, into his own home and providing for their education.

In a word, while they have deservedly earned the acclaim of history, these men exhibited both the goodness and the frailty in human nature and reflected the times in which they lived. None of these details, however, whether negative or positive, have relevance for our parable.

6. Winston Churchill, *Memoirs of the Second World War* (New York: Houghton Mifflin Company, 1959), 227.

7. Oswald Chambers, *My Utmost for His Highest* (Grand Rapids, Mich.: Discovery House, 1935), reading for June 27.

8. Ambrose, *Undaunted Courage* (New York: Simon & Schuster, 1996), 404.

9. I am indebted to Don Meares for the phrase, "to become what God created us to become, and do what He calls us to do." See chapter 7, page 171, for the original context of this formulation.

Chapter Two

1. As a general rule of style, I express collective nouns and pronouns with the generic "man(kind)," "he," "his," "him," unless the context requires a more specific designation, such as "he or she" or "his or hers."

2. Jim Klobuchar, "Ade Christenson's teams learned how to carry the ball," *Minneapolis Star Tribune*, August 15, 1993, B3.

3. Quoted by Joel Belz, "The Price of Immorality," *World Magazine* (1 November 1997), 5.

4. Joel H. Metcalf, "True Saintliness," in *The Moral Compass*, ed. William J. Bennett (New York: Simon & Schuster, 1995), 740.

5. Mention of "our congregation" throughout the book refers to the congregation I served as pastor from 1960 to 1982, Trinity Lutheran Church, San Pedro, California. Luthor Nelson was our youth worker for seven years in the 1970s. His sermon "Premeditated Obedience," remains etched in my memory a quarter of a century later as a vivid description of the fundamental mindset of a Christian disciple.

Chapter Three

1. Larry Christenson, ed., *Welcome, Holy Spirit* (Minneapolis: Augsburg Fortress, 1987), 181.

2. Karl Barth, *Church Dogmatics, Vol. III, Part One*, ed. G. W. Bromiley and T. F. Torrance (Edinburgh: T & T Clark), 192. "An approximation of the Christian doctrine of the Trinity [in Genesis 1:26–28] . . . is both nearer the text and does it more justice than . . . an arrogant rejection of [this] exegesis of the early church."

3. Larry Christenson, "Kingdom Dynamics," *Spirit Filled Life Bible, New King James Version*, ed. Jack W. Hayford (Nashville: Thomas Nelson, 1991), 5–6.

4. Other Scriptures in which Jesus promised to be present with His disciples after His ascension into heaven:

"I am going away and [then] *I am coming back to you*" (John 14:28).

"Righteous Father . . . I have made you known to them [my disciples], and will continue to make you known in order that the love you have for me may be in them *and that I myself may be in them*" (John 17:25–26).

5. A further Scripture in which the apostle Paul taught the indwelling presence of Jesus Christ as a pivotal mystery of the faith: "I have become its servant [of the body of Christ] by the commission God gave me to present to you the word of God in its fullness—the mystery that has been kept hidden for ages and generations, but is now disclosed to the saints. To them God has chosen to make known among the Gentiles the glorious riches of this mystery, which is *Christ in you*, the hope of glory" (Colossians 1:25–27).

6. Other Scriptures in which people continued to experience Jesus' presence as an unmistakable reality after He ascended back to heaven:

"As [Saul of Tarsus] journeyed he came near Damascus, and suddenly a light shone around him from heaven. Then he fell to the ground, and heard a voice saying to him, 'Saul, Saul, why are you persecuting Me?' And he said, 'Who are You, Lord?' Then the Lord said, '*I am Jesus*, whom you are persecuting' " (Acts 9:3–5 NKJV).

"The following night *the Lord stood near* Paul and said, 'Take courage! As you have testified about me in Jerusalem, so you must also testify in Rome' " (Acts 23:11).

7. Other Scriptures in which Jesus promised that He would send another Counselor to His disciples:

"If you love me, you will obey what I command. And I will ask the Father, and he will give you *another Counselor to be with you forever*—the Spirit of truth" (John 14:15–17).

"John baptized with water, but in a few days *you will be baptized with the Holy Spirit*" (Acts 1:5).

"When the day of Pentecost came, they were all . . . *filled with the Holy Spirit* and began to speak in other tongues as the Spirit enabled them" (Acts 2:1, 4).

8. Other Scriptures in which people experienced the presence of the Holy Spirit as an unmistakable reality:

"Paul and his companions traveled throughout the region of Phrygia and Galatia, having been *kept by the Holy Spirit* from preaching the word in the province of Asia" (Acts 16:6).

"This salvation, which was first announced by the Lord [Jesus], was confirmed to us by those who heard him. God also testified to it by signs, wonders and various miracles, and *gifts of the Holy Spirit distributed according to his will*" (Hebrews 2:3–4).

9. Charles Sheldon, *In His Steps* (New York: Smithmark Publishers, Inc., updated edition 1992).

10. J. Rodman Williams, *Renewal Theology, Volume 2: Salvation, the Holy Spirit, and Christian Living* (Grand Rapids, Mich.: Academie Books, Zondervan, 1990), 206–07. Williams makes the point, "In the history of the church's reflection on the Holy Spirit there has traditionally been the tendency to subordinate the work of the Spirit to the work of Christ. Despite the orthodox formulation of the *ontological* equality* of the Spirit and the Son, there has tended to be a *functional* subordination. The role of the Holy Spirit in connection with Christ has been viewed largely as applying the benefits of Christ to the believer, whereas His further work in the Pentecostal coming has been seriously neglected. With the emphasis on the former, the Holy Spirit's work has been functionally subordinated to that of Christ, hence a work of applicative instrumentality.† Accordingly, it has been insufficiently recognized that not only does the Spirit point to Christ but also Christ points to the Spirit, and that beyond the Spirit's work in uniting Christ (the area of salvation) is Christ's me-

---

*Equality in being: the Spirit of the same essence (*homoousios*) as the Son, both equally God. Such was the church's formulation in the Nicene Creed.

†On the matter of viewing the Holy Spirit as applicative and instrumental, I would especially call attention to Hendrikus Berkhof's *Doctrine of the Holy Spirit*, where he writes, "This is the main pneumatological trend in ecclesiastical theology. The Spirit is customarily treated in noetical, applicative, subjective terms. He is the power which directs our attention to Christ and opens our eyes to his work. The main result of his work is the awakening of faith in Christ. His work is merely instrumental. . . . So the Spirit is a second reality beside Christ, but entirely subordinate to him, serving in the application of his atoning work" (p. 23). Berkhof expresses dissatisfaction with this long tradition and urges that "the Spirit is far more than an instrumental entity, the subjective reverse at Christ's work." I gladly confess to having received helpful insight from what Berkhof has said in this connection.

diation of the Spirit to others. Indeed, this latter act of mediation, from the Father through the Son, is that climactic act of the sending of the Holy Spirit. This act, presupposing redemption, represents the coming of the Spirit to a redeemed humanity. The nature of this coming—its various aspects, its purpose, and its results—has been given little attention.

"We may be grateful that in the contemporary spiritual renewal the Holy Spirit is being recognized for His unique and distinctive work."

In our parable of the Lewis and Clark expedition, the longstanding theological pattern to which Williams calls attention echoes the mentality of the War Department bureaucrats who could not grasp the genius of Lewis's co-command with Clark, which Lewis insisted on from the beginning.

11. Bernard DeVoto, ed., *The Journals of Lewis and Clark* (New York: Houghton Mifflin, 1953, 1981) 418, 469.

12. DeVoto, *The Journals of Lewis and Clark*, li–lii.

"Lewis was the diplomatic and commercial thinker, Clark the negotiator. Lewis, who went specially to Philadelphia for training in botany, zoology, and celestial navigation, was the scientific specialist; Clark the engineer and geographer, as well as the master of frontier crafts. Both were experienced rivermen but Lewis acknowledged that Clark had greater skill and usually left the management of the boats to him. Clark evidently had the greater gift for dealing with the Indians. But by chance Lewis was alone at two critical encounters with Indians, the Snakes and the Blackfeet, and he handled them with an expertness that no one could have surpassed. Lewis was better educated than Clark and he had a speculative mind; almost all the abstract ideas and philosophical remarks in the journals are his. Both were men of great intelligence, of distinguished intelligence. The entire previous history of North American exploration contains no one who could be called their intellectual equal.

"In fact, intelligence was the principal reason for the success of the expedition, which is also unequaled in American history and hardly surpassed in the history of exploration anywhere. They were masters of every situation and they successfully handled every emergency.

"That the promised equality of command became a fact is evident. But it is also evident that if there had been any occasion to interrupt it, by personality and temperament Lewis was the natural commander and Clark the adjutant. *There never was an occasion* [italics added]; the two agreed and worked together with a mutuality unknown elsewhere in the history of exploration and rare in any kind of human association."

13. From "The Athanasian Creed," quoted from the version in *The Book of Concord*, trans. and ed. by Theodore G. Tappert (Philadelphia: Fortress Press, 1959), 19.

14. Jörg Erb, *Geduld und Glaube der Heiligen* (Kassel, Germany: Johannes Stauda Verlag, 1965), 79. "Vater, ich danke dir, daß du mich geschaffen hast; Jesu Christe, ich danke dir, daß du mich erlöst hast; heiliger Geist, ich danke dir, daß du mich gereinigt hast. Heilige Dreifaltigkeit sende mir einen barmherzigen Tod, der mich erlöst aus aller Not."

Chapter Four

1. Ambrose, *Undaunted Courage*, 105.

2. David Pawson, *The Normal Christian Birth* (London: Hodder & Stoughton, 1989), 11.

    Pawson states his thesis as follows: "*Christian initiation is a complex of four elements—repenting towards God, believing in the Lord Jesus, being baptised in water and receiving the Holy Spirit.* Each of these is quite distinct from the others. All of them are essential to entering the kingdom of God. They are not mutually exclusive, but are fully complementary and together constitute the process of 'becoming a Christian.' They may occur very close together or over a period of time. The important thing is their *completion* rather than their *coincidence.*" [italics his] He recognizes the significance of the Christian fellowship (our fifth "link"), but does not include it as a formal part of his study.

    Pawson's work in this book, as well as in his subsequent book, *Jesus Baptises in One Holy Spirit*, offers a well thought out synthesis of sacramental, evangelical, and Pentecostal perspectives on the pattern of Christian initiation that is found in the New Testament. Despite some theological differences with him, I find his work extremely useful. Particularly helpful is Pawson's view that "these three streams [sacramental, evangelical, Pentecostal] are right in what they affirm but wrong in what they tend to undervalue, ignore, or even deny."

    Note: When I refer to Pawson's work in the endnotes, I preserve the British spelling of *baptise*, as well as the British spelling of some other words; in the text, we follow American spelling throughout, for example, *baptize*.

3. Søren Kierkegaard's Journals and Papers, Vol. 1, A–E, ed. and trans. by Howard V. Hong and Edna H. Hong (Bloomington and London: Indiana University Press, 1967), 433–34.

4. This characterization means to affirm the positive value of *forensic justifi-*

cation (understanding salvation as the gracious imputation of Christ's righteousness to a believer, through no work or merit of his or her own). This emphasis has been particularly strong in my own Lutheran tradition. "Salvation by grace through faith" is the cornerstone of the Bible's teaching on salvation. If, however, forensic justification is not wedded to a lively understanding of the indwelling presence of Christ, then living the Christian life and growing in Christian character—*sanctification*—become all too easily a matter of human striving, rather than *God working in you to will and to act according to his good purpose* (Philippians 2:13).

5. Larry Christenson, *What About Baptism?* (St. Paul, Minn.: International Lutheran Renewal Center, 1993), 6.

6. Other Scriptures that indicate "receiving the Holy Spirit" had the character of an objective experience:

"Peter and John placed their hands on them, and they received the Holy Spirit. Simon *saw* that the Holy Spirit was given at the laying on of the apostles' hands" (Acts 8:17–18).

"Did you receive the Spirit by observing the law, or by believing what you heard? (Galatians 3:2).

7. George T. Montague and Kilian McDonnell, *Christian Initiation and Baptism in the Holy Spirit: Evidence from the First Eight Centuries* (Collegeville, Minn.: The Liturgical Press, 1991).

8. Tim Dowley, ed., *The History of Christianity* (New York: Guideposts, 1977), 517.

9. "General William Booth Enters Heaven," in *Collected Poems by Vachel Lindsay* (New York: Macmillan Company, 1923), 123–25.

General William Booth Enters Into Heaven
by Vachel Lindsay
(To be sung to the tune of "The Blood of the Lamb" with indicated instrument)

(Bass drum beaten loudly.)
Booth led boldly with his big bass drum—
(Are you washed in the blood of the Lamb?) Hallelujah
Saints smiled gravely and they said: "He's come."
(Are you washed in the blood of the Lamb?)
Walking lepers followed rank on rank,
Lurching bravoes from the ditches dank,
Drabs from the alleyways and drug fiends pale—
Minds still passion-ridden, soul-powers frail:—
Vermin-eaten saints with moldy breath,
Unwashed legions with the ways of Death—
(Are you washed in the blood of the Lamb?)

(Banjos.)
> Every slum had sent its half-a-score
> The round world over. (Booth had groaned for more.)
> Every banner that the wide world flies
> Bloomed with glory and transcendent dyes.
> Big-voiced lasses made their banjos bang,
> Tranced fanatical they shrieked and sang:—
> "Are you washed in the blood of the Lamb?"
> Hallelujah! It was queer to see
> Bull-necked convicts with that land make free.
> Loons with trumpets blowed a blare, blare, blare
> On, on, upward thro' the golden air!
> (Are you washed in the blood of the Lamb?)

(Bass drum slower and softer.)
> Booth died blind and still by faith he trod,
> Eyes still dazzled by the ways of God.
> Booth led boldly, and he looked the chief
> Eagle countenance in sharp relief,
> Beard a-flying, air of high command
> Unabated in that holy land.

(Sweet flute music.)
> Jesus came from out the courthouse door,
> Stretched his hands above the passing poor.
> Booth saw not, but led his queer ones there
> Round and round the mighty courthouse square.
> Yet in an instant all that blear review
> Marched on spotless, clad in raiment new.
> The lame were straightened, withered limbs uncurled
> And blind eyes opened on a new sweet world.

(Bass drum louder)
> Drabs and vixens in a flash made whole!
> Gone was the weasel-head, the snout, the jowl!
> Sages and sibyls now, and athletes clean,
> Rulers of empires, and of forests green!

(Grand chorus of all instruments. Tambourines to the foreground.)
> The hosts were sandalled, and their wings were fire!
> (Are you washed in the blood of the Lamb?)
> But their noise played havoc with the angel-choir.
> (Are you washed in the blood of the Lamb?)
> Oh, shout Salvation! It was good to see
> Kings and Princes by the Lamb set free.
> The banjos rattled and the tambourines
> Jin-jing-jingled in the hands of Queens.

(Reverently sung, no instruments)

And when Booth halted by the curb for prayer
He saw his Master thro' the flag-filled air.
Christ came gently with a robe and crown
For Booth the soldier, while the throng knelt down.
He saw King Jesus. They were face to face,
And he knelt a-weeping in that holy place.
Are you washed in the blood of the Lamb?

10. David Pawson, *Jesus Baptises in One Holy Spirit* (London: Hodder & Stoughton, 1997), 130.

11. Ibid., 187.

12. Pawson, *The Normal Christian Birth*, 27.

13. Agnes Sanford, *The Healing Light* (St. Paul, Minn.: Macalaster Park Publishing Company, 22nd edition, 1957), 120–29.

14. Ibid., 121.

15. Arthur Richter, in conversation with this writer in 1964.

16. Philip Max Johnson, "Exposed by the Light: Confessing Our Sin and Naming Our Sins," *Lutheran Forum* (Fall 1997), an issue titled "Whatever Happened to Private Confession," 15–16. Johnson, pastor of St. Paul Lutheran Church, Jersey City, New Jersey, writes:

"The devil loves generalizations and abstractions, the land of shadows where the contour of our sins remains vague, undefined, unnamed. If our sins are to be exposed to God's light where they squirm and wither, we need to name them aloud.

"There is only one place to begin if this true 'conversation and consolation of the brethren' is to be recovered. It will start with pastors; but I do not mean their teaching. It is a great mistake for pastors to think that if only they trot out a few biblical passages, a few sentences from the confessions, and some lively words from Luther, the congregation will rush to the confessional. The resistance is too strong. No doubt, antinomianism [disdain or dismissal of rules and laws] and anti-catholicism play a large role in this resistance. There is also the Lutheran habit of talking about the Christian life largely in the abstract, fearing that specifics will lead to legalism! And certainly we should not overestimate the eagerness of our parishioners to rush toward the light of God's judgment!

"No doubt the pastor must teach. But the recovery of confession does not *begin* with the pastor's teaching. It begins with the pastor's repentance and penitential practice. Only the truly repentant can convincingly preach repentance. Only the true penitent can teach penance.

Only the confessor of sins can hear confessions. Until the ministerium is something other than a roster of licensed professionals, until we pastors are a fellowship of penitents, knowing among ourselves that true conversation and consolation of the Gospel, private and individual Confession and Absolution will remain an arcane practice here and there among a few confessional throw-backs.

"If, as a pastor, I desire to lead my congregation in the recovery of a fruitful penitential practice, there is one place to begin. I must go and kneel before a confessor, confess my sins to God and beg for that glorious life-bearing Word: 'I forgive your sins in the Name of the Father, and of the Son, and of the Holy Spirit.' "

17. See Larry Christenson, "Private Confession" in *Back to Square One* (Minneapolis: Bethany House Publishers, 1979), 111–20.

18. Pawson, *The Normal Christian Birth*, 258–67.

19. Frank Seilhamer, past president of Hamma Divinity School (Lutheran), in conversation with Larry Christenson and others.

20. "Only Jesus/Calvary's Love," words and music by Greg Nelson and Phill McHugh. Sung by Charles Haugabrooks on CD, *God's Touch Through You*, P.O. Box 244, Tangerine, Florida 32777.

21. Delbert Rossin, in a message at the Southern California Lutheran Conference on the Holy Spirit, 1980. Rossin uses the term *salvation* according to its commonly understood meaning of obtaining forgiveness and the promise of heaven, which is narrower than often found, for example, in the writings of Martin Luther. In the Small Catechism, expounding on the Eucharist, Luther says that by "the words 'for you' and 'for the forgiveness of sins,' the forgiveness of sins, life, and salvation are given to us in the sacrament, for where there is forgiveness of sins, there also is life and salvation." [*The Book of Concord*, trans. and ed. by Theodore G. Tappert (Philadelphia: Fortress Press, 1959), 352.] Danish theologian Regin Prenter expounds on this understanding in Luther with some force: "The forgiveness of sin is first seen in its proper light when it is placed in the all-embracing perspective which stretches from the creation to the consummation. The forgiveness in the *Large Catechism* is, therefore, not seen from the narrow horizon of human piety as something which is necessary in order to give the restless and religious soul 'peace.' " [Regin Prenter, *Spiritus Creator: Luther's Concept of the Holy Spirit* (Philadelphia: Fortress Press, 1953), 244.] This emphasis in Luther underscores the very point Rossin was making, contrasting the popular (but narrow) meaning of "salvation" with the intrinsically wider mean-

ing that one finds in Luther, based on his reading of Scripture.

22. See "The Theology of the Cross," in *Welcome, Holy Spirit*, 190–94, for a critique of the false dichotomy sometimes posed between "faith" and "experience."

23. Martin Luther, *A Commentary on St. Paul's Epistle to the Galatians*, ed. Philip S. Watson (Westwood, New Jersey: Fleming H. Revell Company, 1953), 134.

24. Tuomo Mannermaa, "Why Is Luther So Fascinating? Modern Finnish Luther Research" in *Union with Christ*.

Mannermaa and his colleagues in The New Finnish School of Luther Research show that Martin Luther's profound grasp of the apostle Paul comes to a focus in the understanding that "Christ is not only the object of faith but is himself present in faith" (p. 6). Similar findings came out of the research of the international Lutheran charismatic theological consultation that published *Welcome, Holy Spirit*.

Participants from these two groups had an informal consultation November 20, 1998, in Helsinki, Finland. They had no previous contact with each other, but their research produced similar conclusions. For example, in *Welcome, Holy Spirit*:

"Luther recognized that true faith is not something that springs up from within ourselves. It is created as a gift of God; through the working of the Holy Spirit, Christ is received as the living, redeeming Lord. He recognized that this was a radical break with the common understanding of faith.

"How do people today understand and use the word *faith*? According to common usage, *faith* refers to an innate ability, that is, *something that comes from within myself*: I am the subject, the one who has faith; I place this faith of mine in God, who is the object of my faith.

"Luther understood faith as going beyond a strict subject–object relationship to a point of dynamic identification of subject and object. In one of his writings we virtually see this development taking place:

'Faith, if it be true faith, is a sure trust and confidence of the heart, and a firm consent whereby Christ is apprehended: so that Christ is the object of faith. *Yea rather, He is not the object, but, as it were, in the faith itself Christ is present.*' (Luther's *Commentary on Galatians*)

"The gift of faith is inseparable from the gift of Christ Himself. Apart from the experience of Christ as the living Lord, mediated by the Holy Spirit, all talk of faith is imitation and illusion" (142–43).

25. This section is adapted from "Practicing the Presence of Jesus," in *The*

Christian Family by Larry Christenson (Minneapolis: Bethany House Publishers, 1970), 141–48.

26. Agnes Sanford, in her book *The Healing Light*, which I read during my final year in seminary. It prompted me to undertake a serious study of the revival of the ministry of healing in the Anglican communion, which began in the 1930s.

27. Jim Schmidt was an elder in Trinity Lutheran Church, San Pedro, California, during the 1960s and 1970s.

28. Andrew Murray, *The Spirit of Christ* (Minneapolis: Bethany House Publishers, 1979), 13–14, 16. "The Spirit's work in convincing of sin and of righteousness, in His leading to repentance and faith and the new life, is but the preparatory work. The distinctive glory of the dispensation of the Spirit is His divine personal indwelling in the heart of the believer, there to reveal the Father and the Son. It is only as Christians understand and remember this, that they will be able to claim the full blessing prepared for them in Christ Jesus." (pp. 13–14)

"When the standard of spiritual life in a Church is sickly and low, when neither in the preaching of the word nor in the testimony of believers, the glorious truth of an Indwelling Spirit is distinctly proclaimed, we must not wonder that even where God gives His Spirit, He will be known and experienced only as the Spirit of regeneration. His Indwelling Presence will remain a mystery. In the gift of God, the Spirit of Christ in all His fullness is bestowed once for all as an Indwelling Spirit; but He is received and possessed only as far as the faith of the believer reaches." (pp. 15–16)

29. Pawson, *Jesus Baptises in One Holy Spirit*, 189. Pawson adds, "There is some analogy here with the experience of the twelve apostles: 'he has been *with* you and will be *in* you' (John 14:17). What we must not assume is that this work means either that he has already been 'received' or that he already 'indwells'. Both these terms are kept for Spirit baptism in the New Testament, and should be today. Paul's question is still valid: " 'Having believed, did you receive the Holy Spirit?' " (Acts 19:2).

30. Pawson, *The Normal Christian Birth*, 137.

31. See, for example, J. Rodman Williams, *Renewal Theology, Volume 2: Salvation, the Holy Spirit, and Christian Living* (Grand Rapids, Mich.: Academie Books, Zondervan, 1990), 341–42, 408. Williams shows in a careful study of 1 Corinthians 12–14 (including special treatment of 12:31) that speaking in tongues was accorded a place of high value in

the apostolic church. He decisively lays to rest the pejorative designation of tongues as "the least of the gifts."

See also Montague and McDonnell, *Christian Initiation and Baptism in the Holy Spirit*, 2nd edition, 369. While Roman Catholic scholar Kilian McDonnell does not support the Pentecostal position of tongues being the only "initial evidence" of Spirit baptism, he states that tongues, as an evidence of Spirit baptism, clearly occupies a *privileged place* in the New Testament. (See appendix 4 of this book, "Extended Comment on the 'Release' of the Holy Spirit.")

32. Krister Stendahl, *Paul Among Jews and Gentiles* (Philadelphia: Fortress Press, 1976), 111.
33. The following section is adapted from Larry Christenson, *Speaking in Tongues* (Minneapolis: Bethany House Publishers, 20th printing, 1987), 130–32.
34. Marilyn Hickey, "Knowing God's Will," *Spirit Led Woman*, February/March 1999, 40.
35. Risto Santala, *Armolahjoisra armon tasolta* (Helsinki: Karas–Sana Oy, 1978), 80–89. In this Finnish publication Santala reports his linguistic analysis and a translation of a recording of several glossolalia utterances that Larry Christenson recorded one morning in 1963 during his private devotions, at the request of a research team from the American Lutheran Church that was visiting his congregation in San Pedro, California. A detailed summary of Santala's findings is included in *Welcome, Holy Spirit*, ed. Larry Christenson, Footnote 9, 409–11.
36. Murray, *The Spirit of Christ*, 89.
37. Arthur Richter, director of the *Marburger Kreis*, concluding remarks at a conference in Enkenbach, Germany, 24 August 1963.
38. Murray, *The Spirit of Christ*, 169.

Chapter Five

1. DeVoto, *The Journals of Lewis and Clark*, lv.
2. G. K. Chesterton, "The Paradoxes of Christianity," *Prophet of Orthodoxy: the Wisdom of G. K. Chesterton* (London: Fount/Harper Collins, 1997), 276.
3. D. G. Kehl, "Worship, For the Purpose of Godliness," chapter 5 in *Spiritual Disciplines for the Christian Life*, ed. Donald S. Whitney (Colorado Springs, Colo.: Navpress, 1991), 89. Adapted from Kehl's *Control Yourself! Practicing the Art of Self-Discipline*.

4. Bill Bright, at Arrowhead Springs, California, in a talk to a men's retreat from Trinity Lutheran Church, San Pedro, California, 23 May 1964.

Chapter Six

1. Paul Johnson, *A History of the American People* (New York: Harper Perennial, 1999), 471.
2. Murray, *The Spirit of Christ*, 172–73, 175.
3. "The Smalcald Articles," *The Book of Concord*, trans. and ed. by Theodore G. Tappert (Philadelphia: Fortress Press, 1959), 310.
4. Carl von Clausewitz, *Principles of War*, trans. by Hans Gatzke (Harrisburg, Penn.: The Military Service Publishing Company, 1942), 26.
5. The three-year program of Bible teaching that we developed for young people is published by Bethany House Publishers, Minneapolis, as the *Trinity Bible Series*. It uses *Hurlbut's Story of the Bible* as a basic text. We had read through this book three times in our own family devotions. Our children never seemed to tire of hearing it. The series includes a workbook for each year's study—two covering the Old Testament, one the New Testament: *The Covenant, The Kingdom, Christ and His Church*. The workbooks help the students underline and mark up their textbooks, highlighting basic biblical teachings. Sandra Hall's *Teacher's Guide* includes a variety of helps for each lesson—visual aids, projects, discussion questions, etc.

   Hurlbut's telling of the Bible stories is free of doctrinal bias. The *Trinity Bible Series* is used by a variety of Christian groups and denominations. In our congregation it served as a program for Lutheran confirmation instruction. Aside from the material itself, the most notable innovation for our people was that we lowered the age of confirmation instruction, beginning it in the fourth grade rather than the seventh grade. Sister Lucia, from the Evangelical Sisterhood of Mary, in Darmstadt, Germany, was living in our congregation the year we began this program. Her father, Jörg Erb, a German educator, wrote us: "I have pled for years with our church authorities in Germany to do what you are doing—change the age of confirmation instruction. From an educational standpoint, age 13 or 14 (seventh or eighth grade) is positively the *worst* age to do it—it should be done either earlier (as you are doing), or later, in the upper years of high school." His comment proved absolutely true to our experience. Discipline problems plummeted. The children surprised us with how well they could handle basic biblical material. They obtained a foundational knowledge of Scripture and formed close friendships that significantly helped them as they moved into the sometimes difficult transitional years of junior high school.

Confirmation instruction for young people is a strong tradition in the Lutheran church. Even families that have only minimal involvement in the life of a congregation make certain that their children are confirmed. It presents a wonderful opportunity to reach young people, but it has a downside that is almost universal in Lutheran congregations worldwide: following confirmation, many young people drift away from the church. We saw this trend reverse when our young people became involved with serious Bible study and Christian fellowship at a younger age.

6. See Acts 15:28; 4:31; 5:3–5; 8:14–17; 27:22–24.

Chapter Seven

1. Andrew Murray, *The Spirit of Christ*, 179–80.
2. Stephen Ambrose, lecture at the Charles Russell Museum, Great Falls, Montana, 27 June 1997.
3. Don Meares, *Grace: the Empowering Presence of God*, six audio cassettes, published by Don Meares Ministry, 13901 Central Avenue, Upper Marlboro, Maryland 20774.

   His biblical study of *grace* rests on two legs: etymology and theology. He recognizes the idea of "favor" in the etymology of the word. He also underscores the classical meaning, that God's "graciousness is always God's free gift." (Gerhard Kittel, *Theological Dictionary of the New Testament* [Grand Rapids, Mich.: Wm. B. Eerdmans, 1964], Vol. IX, 378.)

   In the New Testament, Meares points out, God's favor goes beyond giving believers a "something" called "grace." God shows His favor by giving *himself*. This accords with the nuance cited in Kittel, that in the New Testament, *charis* ("grace") shows affinity to the ordinary use of *pneuma* ("Spirit"). *Charis* can depict the Spirit-filled man (Kittel, 392).

   Thus, the central thrust of the New Testament meaning of *grace* is not simply "favor" but *presence*. God shows His favor by and through *His empowering presence* in the life of the believer.
4. The example that follows is adapted from "The Old Landlord," by Larry Christenson in *The Renewed Mind* (Minneapolis: Bethany House Publishers, 1974), 41–52.
5. Chambers, *My Utmost for His Highest*, reading for May 29.
6. Ibid., reading for March 20.

Appendix One

1. *"Opera Dei ad extra indivisa sunt, ad intra divisa sunt."*
2. Robert W. Jenson, *The Triune Identity* (Philadelphia: Fortress Press, 1982), 21.
3. McGrath, *Understanding the Trinity*, 148, 115.
4. Pawson, *The Normal Christian Birth*, 325–27.
5. See, for example, J. Rodman Williams, *Renewal Theology, Vol. 1* (Grand Rapids, Mich.: Academie Books, Zondervan Publishing House, 1988), 91–92.
6. Karl Barth. *Church Dogmatics, Vol III, Part One*, ed. Bromiley & Torrance (Edinburgh: T & T Clark), 192.
7. Jenson, *The Triune Identity*, 146.

Appendix Two

1. See *The Pentecostals* by Walter Hollenweger (Minneapolis: Augsburg Publishing, 1972), 514–15.
2. See Vinson Synan, *The Holiness-Pentecostal Movement in the United States* (Grand Rapids, Mich.: William B. Eerdmans, 1971), 115–16.
3. Pawson, *Jesus Baptises in One Holy Spirit*, 36, 118.
4. Jacob Tanner, "Baptism: A Ceremony? Or, A Means of Grace?" *Book Mission Tract No. 137* (Minneapolis: Augsburg Publishing, Book Mission of The Evangelical Lutheran Church, 1939), 10.
5. Gerhard Kittel, *Theological Dictionary of the New Testament, Vol. I* (Grand Rapids, Mich.: Wm. B. Eerdmans, 1964), 719ff. In the German edition, Kittel combines the Greek transliteration, *glossolalia*, with the German term *Zungenreden* ("speaking in tongues"), coming up with *Glossenreden*, as a device to help convey the idea that the New Testament Greek, *en glossais lalein*, is a "technical term."
6. Robert Jenson, "Eighth Locus: The Holy Spirit" in *Christian Dogmatics, Volume 2* (Philadelphia: Fortress Press, 1984), 119.
7. Pawson, *Jesus Baptises in One Holy Spirit*, 185–87.
8. William Martin, *A Prophet with Honor: The Billy Graham Story* (New York: William Morrow, Quill, 1991), 98–99.
9. Billy Graham, *Just as I Am* (San Francisco: HarperCollins/Zondervan, 1997), 111.
10. Pawson, *Jesus Baptises in One Holy Spirit*, 197–98.
11. James Ackerman, pastor in the Lutheran Church-Missouri Synod in conversation, during a theological seminar in Chicago, 27 October 1997.

Appendix Three

1. Larry Christenson, *Speaking in Tongues: A Gift for the Body of Christ* (Minneapolis: Lutheran Renewal Center, 1963, 1990), 4.
2. See *Welcome, Holy Spirit*, Larry Christenson, ed. (Minneapplis: Augsburg, 1987) note 1, 408.

Appendix Four

1. Kallistos Ware, Bishop of Diokleia, "Personal Experience of the Holy Spirit According to the Greek Fathers," paper presented at an ecumenical theological conference in Prague, Czech Republic, 12 September 1997.
2. *Fanning the Flame: What Does Baptism in the Holy Spirit Have to Do with Christian Initiation?* eds. Kilian McDonnell and George Montague (Collegeville, Minn.: The Liturgical Press, 1991), 26.
3. Larry Christenson, *The Charismatic Renewal Among Lutherans* (St. Paul, Minn.: International Lutheran Renewal Center, 1976, 1985), 50–51. See also, Larry Christenson, *What About Baptism?* (Minneapolis: Augsburg Publishing, 1986), 18.
4. "Pray for the Power of the Holy Spirit," tract published by *Renewal in Missouri*, an association of pastors and laity in the Lutheran Church-Missouri Synod.
5. James D. G. Dunn, *Baptism in the Holy Spirit* (Philadelphia: The Westminster Press, 1970), 66.
6. Frederick Dale Bruner, *A Theology of the Holy Spirit* (Grand Rapids, Mich.: William B. Eerdmans, 1970), 178.
7. George T. Montague and Kilian McDonnell, *Christian Initiation and Baptism in the Holy Spirit: Evidence From the First Eight Centuries* (Collegeville, Minn.: The Liturgical Press, 1991), 34–35.
8. *Luther's Works, American Edition, Volume 33*, "Bondage of the Will" (St. Louis: Concordia, 1963), 162–63.

SUBJECT INDEX

SCRIPTURE INDEX